"Here is a uniquely fresh, accessible, and truly original contribution to the field. Jennifer van Sijll takes her readers in a wholly new direction, integrating aspects of screenwriting with all the film crafts in a way I've never before seen. She underscores cinema's collaborative nature, and celebrates the collective family of film artists who struggle together in the creation of worthy movies. It is essential reading not only for screenwriters but also for filmmakers of every stripe."

— Prof. Richard Walter, UCLA Screenwriting Chairman

"A powerful and evocative guide for screenwriters and filmmakers alike."

— Frank Beddor , Producer, *There's Something About Mary*

"After taking Jennifer's class I rewrote the first thirty pages of my screenplay like a madman, without lifting the pen from the paper. Her book and lectures have had a profound effect on me as a filmmaker and as a screenwriting teacher. Her concepts of cinematic storytelling are brilliantly laid out and will be a source of inspiration for future screenwriters and filmmakers."

— Michael Tierno, author of *Aristotle's Poetics for Screenwriters* and award winning writer-director of feature films

"Wow! A screenwriting book with an original and insightful approach. Jennifer van Sijll takes you step by step through the complex transfer from blank page to motion picture. I can finally show a book to my mother and say 'This is what I do for a living.'"

— Larry Karaszewski, Golden Globe-winning screenwriter of *Ed Wood* and *The People vs Larry Flynt*

"Ms. Van Sijll breaks down years of film school into one magnificent book. Three cheers for this clear-cut and extraordinary work."

— Libby Hinson, two-time Emmy winner, Humanitas nominee, winner of the 2004 New York Film Festival Award

"A valuable contribution to the art of storytelling. A must read."

— Michael MacMillan, Producer *CSI: Miami, CSI:NY, CSI: Crime Scene Investigation*; CEO Alliance Atlantis Communications

"For anyone serious about writing and directing."

— P .J. Haarsma, writer of *The Softwire Series*

"*Cinematic Storytelling*, as its name implies, conveys, in visual images, the most essential, most effective cinematic techniques directors and cinematographers use to tell stories. Employing classic images and accompanying text from some of the most memorable scenes in some of the most innovative films in recent times, the book is an instructive visual feast for everyone who aspires to effectively tell great stories with compelling images. Highly recommended."

— Jeffrey M. Freedman, Screenwriter, Author

"This is the preeminent text for any screenwriter who is seriously thinking about directing their own screenplay. By blending classic and contemporary references, Van Sijll plants the seeds for a new generation of auteurs."

— Catherine Clinch, *Creative Screenwriting*

"Jennifer van Sijll's book makes a direct hit in terms of concise information and perfectly chosen visuals, but it also searches out an emotional core that many books of this nature either miss or are afraid of... this book finds it."

— Kirsten Sheridan, co-writer, *In America*, director, *Disco Pigs*

"A smart, analytical guide. Van Sijll truly understands what makes great movies work. A first-rate roadmap and a veritable tour de force of succinct writing."

> — Jake Eberts, Executive Producer, *The Name of the Rose, Hope and Glory, Driving Miss Daisy, Dances with Wolves, A River Runs Through It, Chicken Run*

"Jennifer van Sijll tackles with brio the difficult task of explaining cinematic language which, in its broad acceptance, has become today's most powerful means of communication. The force of this excellent educational tool, with its pertinent and crystalline examples, lies in its ability to convey the specific way in which this singular medium produces meaning."

> — Bruno Toussaint, author of *Le Langage des Images et des Sons* and professor at the Université de Marne la Vallée and ESRA, Paris.

"*Cinematic Storytelling* shows you how a story idea is realized in script form and then transformed again when it moves from script to screen. It underscores how this process necessitates the collaborative relationship between writers and directors. Van Sijll has written an essential guide for aspiring writers and directors."

> — Mardik Martin, Screenwriter, *Raging Bull, Mean Streets, New York, New York*, Senior Lecturer of Screenwriting at USC.

"Van Sijll challenges the notion of writing as limited to the Aristotelian staples of character, structure, and plot. Her book *Cinematic Storytelling* delivers a foundation for the understanding of a new form of literacy, as important as reading and writing with words. Every writing class should add this book to their assigned reading list."

> — David Tamés, Program Director, Digital Filmmaking, The Center for Digital Imaging Arts at Boston University

CINEMATIC STORYTELLING

THE 100 MOST POWERFUL FILM CONVENTIONS

EVERY FILMMAKER MUST KNOW

JENNIFER VAN SIJLL

Published by Michael Wiese Productions
3940 Laurel Canyon Blvd.
Suite #1111
Studio City, CA 91604
(818) 379-8799, (818) 986-3408 (FAX).
mw@mwp.com
www.mwp.com

Cover design by MWP
Interior design by William Morosi
Copyedited by Paul Norlen
Printed by

Manufactured in the United States of America
Copyright 2005 Jennifer Van Sijll

Library of Congress Cataloging-in-Publication Data

Van Sijll, Jennifer, 1954-
  Cinematic storytelling : the 100 most powerful film
conventions every filmmaker must know / Jennifer Van Sijll.
     p. cm.
  ISBN 1-932907-05-X
  1. Cinematography. 2. Motion pictures--Production and direction. I.
Title.
  TR850.V36 2005
  791.4302'33--dc22

2004024722

CONTENTS

Acknowledgments   viii

Preface: Cinematic Storytelling   x

Introduction   xi

   Cinematic Storytelling: The Screenwriter   xi

      The Problem   xi

      What Does This Mean for the Screenwriter?   xi

      Script Excerpts   xi

   Cinematic Storytelling: The Director   xii

      The Problem   xii

      What Does This Mean for the Director?   xii

1. Space: 2-D & 3-D Screen Direction

1. Space: 2-D & 3-D Screen Direction		1
Introduction		2
1. X-Axis (Horizontal)	*Strangers on a Train*	4
2. Y-Axis (Vertical)	*Strangers on a Train*	6
3. XY-Axes (Diagonals)	*Metropolis, The Piano*	8
4. Z-Axis (Depth-of-Field)	*Citizen Kane*	10
5. Z-Axis (Planes of Action)	*Dolores Claiborne*	12
6. Z-Axis (Rack Focus)	*The Graduate*	14
2. Frame: Composition		17
Introduction		18
7. Directing the Eye	*Citizen Kane*	20
8. Imbalance	*Disco Pigs*	22
9. Balance	*Disco Pigs*	24
10. Orientation	*Apocalypse Now, Barton Fink*	26
11. Size	*Metropolis*	29
3. Shape Within the Frame		31
Introduction		32
12. Circular	*The Conversation*	34
13. Linear	*Fargo*	36
14. Triangular	*Witness*	38
15. Rectangular	*The Searchers*	40
16. Organic versus Geometric	*Witness*	42
4. Editing: Pudovkin's Five Editing Techniques		45
Introduction: A Little Theory		46
Five Editing Principles		46
"On Editing"		46
Editing: Additional Techniques		47
17. Montage	*Citizen Kane*	48
18. Montage	*Adaptation*	50
19. Assembly	*Psycho*	52
20. Mise-en-Scène	*Psycho*	54
21. Intercutting	*Cabaret*	56
22. Split Screen	*Kill Bill Vol. 1*	58
23. Dissolves	*Citizen Kane*	60
24. Dissolves	*Barton Fink*	62
25. Smash Cut	*American Beauty*	64
5. Time		67
Introduction		68
26. Expanding Time through Pacing	*Barton Fink*	70
27. Contrast of Time (Pacing and		

	Intercutting)	*Pulp Fiction*	72
28.	Expanding Time — Overlapping Action	*Pulp Fiction*	74
29.	Slo-Motion	*Raging Bull*	76
30.	Fast-Motion (Time Compression)	*Amélie*	78
31.	Flashback	*Sunset Boulevard*	80
32.	Flashforward	*The People vs. Larry Flynt*	82
33.	Freeze-Frame	*Butch Cassidy and the Sundance Kid, Thelma and Louise, The 400 Blows*	84
34.	Visual Foreshadowing	*The Piano*	86

6. Sound Effects

			89
	Introduction		90
35.	Realistic Sound (Diegetic) (Character)	*Klute*	92
36.	Realistic Sound (Diegetic) (Emotional Response)	*ET*	94
37.	Expressive Sound (Diegetic) (Outer World)	*Barton Fink*	96
38.	Surreal Sound (Meta-Diegetic) (Inner World)	*Barton Fink*	98

7. Music

			101
39.	Lyrics as Narrator	*Apocalypse Now*	102
40.	Symbolic Use of Music	*Shawshank Redemption*	104
41.	Music as a Moveable Prop	*Out of Africa*	106

8. Scene Transitions (Audio and Visual)

			109
	Introduction		110
42.	Matching Audio Segue	*Sorry, Wrong Number, Fatal Attraction*	112
43.	Audio Bridge (Dialog)	*Citizen Kane*	114
44.	Audio Bridge (Sound Effects)	*Barton Fink*	116
45.	Visual Match-Cut (Graphic Similarity)	*Single White Female*	118
46.	Visual Match-Cut (Pattern and Color)	*Citizen Kane*	120
47.	Visual Match-Cut (Action)	*2001: A Space Odyssey*	122
48.	Visual Match-Cut (Idea)	*Requiem for a Dream*	124
49.	Visual Match-Cut (Idea)	*Harold and Maude*	126
50.	Extended Match Dissolve (Time Transition)	*Titanic*	128
51.	Disrupted Match-Cut	*Bound*	130

9. Camera Lenses

			133
52.	Wide-Angle	*Citizen Kane*	134
53.	Wide-Angle (Vistas and Establishing Shots)	*The Piano*	136
54.	Telephoto	*The Graduate*	138
55.	Fisheye	*Requiem for a Dream*	140
56.	Prop Lenses within the Scene (Fisheye)	*Citizen Kane*	142
57.	Objects	*Dances with Wolves*	144

10. Camera Position

			147
58.	Close-up (CU)	*The Piano*	148
59.	Extreme Close-up (ECU)	*Kill Bill Vol. 1*	150
60.	Two-Shot	*The Piano*	152
61.	Over-the-Shoulder Shot (OTS)	*Chinatown, The Piano*	154
62.	Point-of-View (POV)	*Halloween*	156
63.	Point-of-View (POV)	*Jaws*	158
64.	High-Angle	*Citizen Kane*	160
65.	Low-Angle	*ET*	162
66.	Hi-Lo Combined	*Psycho*	164

11. Camera Motion   167

67. Static Shot	*Klute*	168
68. Pan	*Dances with Wolves*	170
69. Tilt-Up (Character)	*The Professional*	172
70. Tilt-Down	*Fargo*	174
71. Rotation	*Bound, Apocalypse Now*	176
72. Tracking Shot	*Fatal Attraction*	178
73. Circular	*Reservoir Dogs*	180
74. Push In — Push Out	*Fargo*	182
75. Crane	*Touch of Evil*	184
76. Handheld	*Touch of Evil*	186
77. Handheld	*Pulp Fiction*	188
78. Steadicam	*Goodfellas*	190
79. Aerial	*The Piano*	192

12. Lighting   195

80. Rembrandt Lighting (Light versus Dark)	*Apocalypse Now*	196
81. TV Lighting	*Natural Born Killers*	198
82. Candlelight	*American Beauty*	200
83. Motivated Lighting	*Fatal Attraction*	202
84. Unmotivated Light	*The Professional*	204
85. Motion	*ET*	206

13. Color   209

86. Coding Character	*Three Women*	210

14. Props   213

87. Props (Externalizing Character)	*Barton Fink*	214
88. Props (Externalizing Character)	*Raging Bull*	216
89. Repurposing Props	*Bound*	218
90. Contrast	*Harold and Maude*	220

15. Wardrobe   223

91. Wardrobe	*Ed Wood*	224
92. Repurposing Wardrobe	*Out of Africa*	226
93. Contrast of Wardrobe	*Bound*	228

16. Locations   231

94. Defining Character	*Hedwig and the Angry Inch*	232
95. Location as Unifying Element	*The Sweet Hereafter*	234
96. Location as Theme	*Blue Velvet*	236
97. Moving Locations	*Dead Man*	238

17. Natural Environment   241

Introduction		242
98. Climate	*The Sixth Sense*	244
99. Seasons and the Passage of Time	*Amélie*	246
100. Physical Phenomena	*Dolores Claiborne*	248

ACKNOWLEDGMENTS

I would like to thank my students at San Francisco State and Berkeley Extension for their contribution to the book. They have given me new knowledge and delivered it with great fun and passion. I also want to thank Bill Nichols and Jim Kitses at San Francisco State who gave me my first job teaching film, and Liz McDonough at Berkeley Extension for so warmly embracing my input.

My warmest gratitude goes to my teachers at USC, especially Les Novros, Frank Daniel, Mardik Martin, Mel Sloan, Gene Coe, Mort Zarkoff, Pam Douglas, Trevor Greenwood, Duke Underwood, Herb Pearl, Ken Muira, Bob Miller, Ken Evans, Marsha Kinder, Drew Casper, and Eddie Dmytryk. The inspiration for the book is theirs.

I am especially grateful for the course taught by Les Novros wherein we explored what Les called "the dynamics of the frame." From Les I learned that the subject of the frame was only part of what was messaged to the audience. There were hundreds of elements combining to express ideas, which, when used purposefully, could deliver shadings as subtle as the written text. From Les' teaching I came to realize that to master the craft of filmmaking, one had to understand the relationship between the idea and the full complement of film tools.

I would also like to acknowledge my debt to Margaret Mehring's 1990 book, *Screenplay, A Blend of Film Form and Content*. Mehring was then the Director of USC's undergraduate program called Filmic Writing. For me, Mehring's work was a continuation of the lessons learned in Les' class, but it went further in articulating how the cinematic principles Les had explored could be applied specifically to the screenplay.

Cinematic Storytelling owes a great deal to both Les Novros and Margaret Mehring. My catalog of film elements borrows much from both Les' lectures and Mehring's work as does my approach to screenwriting and filmmaking generally.

I am also indebted to Betty Bamberg of USC who granted me a three-year academic award that enabled me to finance my studies.

Deep thanks goes to Michael Wiese, filmmaker and publisher, for giving shape to *Cinematic Storytelling* and guiding the process with such enthusiasm and warmth. I am indebted to Michael and his team, headed by Ken Lee and assisted by book designer Bill Morosi and editor Paul Norlen. Their talent and dedication gave the book form.

To my good friend Kalynn Huffman Brower at Indiana University–Bloomington, the warmest thanks for her generosity in reading the material and her insightful contributions to the manuscript.

I am also deeply indebted to the writers, directors, and cinematographers whose work is referenced, for sharing their vision and raising the craft of filmmaking to an art.

And finally I want to thank my husband, David, and daughter, Skylar, as well as my family and friends, for their love, support and encouragement.

"I can pick up a screenplay and flip through the pages. If all I see is dialog, dialog, dialog, I won't even read it. I don't care how good the dialog is — it's a moving picture. It has to move all the time.

"Screenwriters do not get the lesson… It's not the stage. A movie audience doesn't have the patience to sit and learn a lesson. Their eyes need to be dazzled. The writer is the most important element in the entire film because if it ain't on the page it ain't going to be on the screen."

— Robert Evans, "The Biggest Mistake Writers Make"

"In many of the films now being made, there is very little cinema: they are mostly what I call 'photographs of people talking.' When we tell a story in cinema, we should resort to dialog only when it's impossible to do otherwise. I always try to tell a story in the cinematic way, through a succession of shots and bits of film in between.

"It seems unfortunate, that with the arrival of sound, the motion picture, overnight, assumed a theatrical form. The mobility of the camera doesn't alter this fact. Even though the camera may move along the sidewalk, it's still theatre.

"One result of this is the loss of cinematic style, and another is the loss of fantasy. In writing a *screenplay*, it is essential to separate clearly the dialog from the visual elements and, whenever possible, to rely more on the visual than on the dialog. Whichever way you choose to stage the action, your main concern is to hold the audience's fullest attention.

"Summing it up, one might say that the screen rectangle must be charged with emotion."

— Alfred Hitchcock (quoted in *Hitchcock* by François Truffaut)

"…(E)diting is not merely a method of the junction of separate scenes or pieces, but it is a method that controls the 'psychological guidance' of the spectator.

"…(C)onstructional editing, a method specifically and peculiarly filmic, is, in the hands of the scenarist, an important instrument of impression. Careful study of its use in pictures, combined with talent, will undoubtedly lead to the discovery of new possibilities and, in conjunction with them, to the creation of new forms."

— Vsevolod Pudovkin, *Film Technique* (1926)

CINEMATIC STORYTELLING

There are hundreds of ways of conveying ideas in movies; dialog is but one. This book has assembled 100 non-dialog techniques, creating a kind of encyclopedia of cinematic storytelling. This "encyclopedia" includes examples from some of the most memorable moments in film history. Although space limits the collection to 100, the hope is that the examples are sufficiently representative to help writers and directors better understand the storytelling potential of the film medium.

Cinematic Storytelling: What is It?

For the first twenty years of film history, cinematic storytelling was the only way to convey story. As sync sound was not yet invented, movies like *The Great Train Robbery*, *Metropolis*, and *The Battleship Potemkin* had to use non-dialog techniques to carry character and plot. Titles cards were used when explanations were necessary, but always as a last resort.

Camera placement, lighting, composition, motion, and editing were relied on as the primary storytellers. Cinematic tools, like the camera, were not just used to record the scene. Instead, they were responsible for advancing plot and character. There was no dialog to default to.

After sound came in 1926, dialog and voice-narration soon appeared in movies. These devices, borrowed from novels and plays, were literary in origin, and were floated on top of the moving picture. Many purists bemoaned the coming of sound, while others saw enhancement. In either case, both storytelling systems were now available to screenwriters and directors.

Literary and Cinematic Storytelling

Despite the arrival of literary storytelling tools, cinematic innovations continued. Films like *Citizen Kane*, *Sunset Boulevard*, *Crossfire*, *Psycho*, *The Piano*, and *Raising Arizona* became textbook cases of their use.

Although cinematic tools favor certain genres such as action, horror, noir, psychological drama, and suspense, even the most literary of directors, Woody Allen, often includes a cinematic race against the clock, somewhere in Act Two and somewhere in Manhattan.

Few how-to-books discuss cinematic writing, which is surprising as most genres depend on it to carry story. Although cinematic storytelling can be obvious, most often it's not. It manipulates our emotions, revealing character and plot without our immediate knowledge. That's also why it can be so effective and engaging. Think of the first ten minutes of *ET*. The set-up is completely cinematic. Not a word of dialog. Yet any eight year-old can tell you who the bad guys are and why. As cinematic storytelling often operates on our subconscious, it is difficult to catch and rarely obvious. But this doesn't diminish the need for screenwriters and directors to become more fluent in its use. Instead, it underscores its importance.

Cinematic storytelling is the difference between documenting and dramatizing, between employing the potent storytelling tools in the medium or leaving them silent. Hopefully, this book will expand the storytelling continuum for developing writers and directors, helping them more fully exploit the inherent tools of the medium.

INTRODUCTION

Cinematic Storytelling: The Screenwriter

The Problem

A script is a blueprint of a cinematic story: one told with sound and picture.

There are two requirements of a great script: One is to have a great story, the other is to render the story cinematically. There is a wealth of excellent books that deal with the first part. These books generally cover plot, structure, and character. These are fundamental issues for any work of fiction. In fact, most of these books could be equally applied to the novel or the play and consequently might more accurately be described as works on dramaturgy, not screenwriting. In either case, they make up the first and very important requirement. The second requirement is to render the story cinematically. Without this the writer might have a great story but it's anyone's guess if it will make a great movie.

Film isn't the same as the novel or the short story. It introduces technical elements that the screenwriter is expected to exploit. Screenwriters' ability to do this is what differentiates them from other writers. Many first-time screenwriters forgo the creative opportunities of the medium, defaulting to dialog and narration instead. When screenwriters abandon cinematic techniques, they leave a lot of their movie behind on the roadside. A successful script needs to be a blueprint of a movie, which includes conveying to the reader what they will see and hear on the screen.

In the early days of film, theorists like Lev Kuleshov, Sergei Eisenstein, and Vsevolod Pudovkin set out to understand the storytelling potential of the new medium. They recognized that film offered two things that no other medium had up to this point: a photographed image and motion. This opened up literally thousands of new options for the screenwriter.

Editing introduced crosscutting which quickly developed a number of dramatic staples, including the chase scene. The camera could go outside. It could juxtapose exterior and interior shots. Images could be brought to the audience from around the globe and from new vantage points like the close-up. Each lens could lend specific visual qualities to an image, and each could be exploited to enhance the story. Camera movement, facilitated by a host of methods such as the crane, and later, the Steadicam, suggested a whole new world of possibilities.

What Does This Mean for the Screenwriter?

Early on, Pudovkin recognized that the job of scenarist would be to write stories that exploited the new medium. In 1926 he advised screenwriters to master the technical aspects of film, such as editing, so that they could better create stories specifically for the screen.

This book is intended to follow the path of the early theorists in championing cinematic storytelling. It includes 100 non-dialog techniques used by some of the industry's top writers and directors. From *Metropolis* to *Kill Bill*, the book illustrates, through more than 500 frame grabs and 76 script excerpts, how the film medium can be exploited to advance story. Hopefully they will demonstrate the value that cinematic writing can lend to a screenplay.

Script Excerpts

The script excerpts are included specifically for the screenwriter. They demonstrate how master screenwriters have incorporated cinematic storytelling into their scripts without disrupting the read or directing-the-director. For this reason scripts from both screenwriters and writer-directors have been included. These include excerpts from writers like Alan Ball, Michael Blake, and Robert Towne, as well as from writer-directors like Quentin Tarantino, Jane Campion, and the Coen Brothers.

The hope is that screenwriters will become more fluent in cinematic storytelling.

Cinematic Storytelling: The Director

The Problem

In teaching filmmaking, story and film are often taught separately. Screenwriters are housed in one building, production people in another. Unintentionally, a divide is created where there should be a bond. Technical tools become separated from their end, which is story.

Movies start and end with story. That's why film is purchased and crews are hired, no other reason. Many high-budget films employ dazzling effects, promising great moviemaking, but are anything but. This is because they have forgotten about story. Story has taken a back seat to technical wizardry and style.

What Does This Mean for the Director?

A master craftsman knows how to create a specific shot, but a director knows why. Part of a director's required knowledge is to understand the technical properties of film and then employ them creatively to advance the story. Without the connection between content and technique, you are watching two disjointed parts; the result, more often than not, is a technical exercise.

Cinematic Storytelling examines the work of Fritz Lang, Orson Welles, Alfred Hitchcock, Francis Coppola, Steven Spielberg, Jane Campion, Tim Burton, the Coen Brothers, Luc Besson, James Cameron, and the Wachowski Brothers, among others. In each example, a specific technique is analyzed for its story contribution. For these directors, and many other great cinematic filmmakers, a shot isn't considered unless it advances plot or character. There are no throwaways.

The first part of the director's job is knowing what the audience should be feeling, and when. The second part is harnessing the tools to get them there.

Cinematic Storytelling attempts to bridge the two disciplines: film production and screenwriting. The hope is to marry form and function by illustrating how some of the top directors have achieved this and, in so doing, created some of the most memorable moments in movie history.

SECTION 1

SPACE

SPACE: 2-D & 3-D SCREEN DIRECTION

Film space refers to the spatial dynamics inherent in the film frame. A film frame is both a static snapshot and part of a moving picture. When coupled with motion, screen direction becomes a powerful story element.

Static Image and Motion

Like a painting, the static image of the frame presents inherent storytelling opportunities. Because a movie is a motion picture, the composition of the frame continuously changes. This added characteristic affords two important story elements — that of screen direction and comparison. Screen direction can suggest antagonism, individualism, and conflict, for example. A moving frame might be used to represent change, similarity or dissimilarity, or its opposite, stasis.

Screen Direction

Screen Direction refers to the direction a character or object is travelling.

X-axis refers to the line that cuts the frame horizontally. Objects can run left-to-right or right-to-left along the X-axis.

Y-axis refers to the line that cuts the frame vertically. Objects can move up or down the Y-axis, that is, from the top of the frame to the bottom and vice-versa.

Z-axis refers to the axis that runs from the foreground-to-the-background or background-to-the-foreground in the frame. The Z-axis is what gives the audience its sense of 3-D space or depth-of-field.

Here's how screen direction expressed six different ideas.

Film Element: Screen Direction

1. X-axis (Horizontal)   (*Strangers on a Train*)   Pending Conflict

2. Y-axis (Vertical)   (*Strangers on a Train*)   Detouring

3. XY-axes (Diagonals)   (*Metropolis, The Piano*)   Descent

4. Z-axis (Depth-of-field)   (*Citizen Kane*)   Separate Time Zones

5. Z-axis (Planes of Action)   (*Dolores Claiborne*)   Change of Size

6. Z-axis (Rack Focus)   (*The Graduate*)   Shifting Perspective

Fig. 1
2-Dimensional Screen Direction

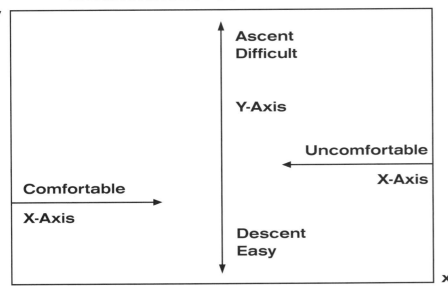

Movement in Flat 2-Dimensional Space

Fig. 2
3-Dimensional Screen Direction

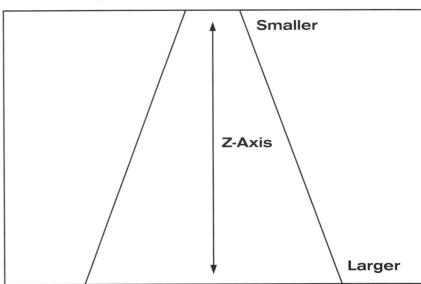

Movement in Depth Along the Z-Axis

X-axis: The eye moves comfortably from left to right as this mimics reading. The eye is less experienced to move the opposite direction and is therefore less comfortable.

Y-axis: Moving an object down the screen appears easy as it is aided by our sense of gravity. Moving an object up the screen will appear difficult because it is assumed it will be resisted by gravity.

Z-axis: When an object moves along the Z-axis the object appears to move in 3-D space moving from front-to-back or back-to-front. Image size will change depending on where the object appears on the trajectory and which lens has been used.

1. Film Element: X-Axis (Horizontal)

Left-to-Right

As Westerners we read left-to-right. If you rented fifty studio-made movies, there's a good chance that the "good guy" will enter screen left every time. When the "good guy" moves left-to-right our eyes move comfortably. Subconsciously, we begin to make positive inferences.

Right-to-Left

Conversely, the antagonist usually enters from the right. Since our eyes aren't used to moving from *right-to-left*, the antagonist's entrance makes us uncomfortable. The screenwriter exploits this by transferring our learned discomfort to the character. The subtle irritant directs audiences to see the character negatively. In the same way we code a black hat as a negative symbol, we can also code screen direction negatively.

Conflict

When these two forces are aimed at each other, we naturally anticipate some kind of collision. Here's how this was exploited in *Strangers on a Train*.

Film Example: *Strangers on a Train*

The opening scene shows a man exiting a cab at a train station. Then it cuts to a second cab and another traveler exiting. Both travelers are shot from the knees down. One wears the two-tone shoes of a dandy, the other, conservative lace-ups.

The dandy walks from right-to-left, the direction associated with the antagonist, while the conservative walks from left-to-right, suggesting he's the protagonist. Then their walk is inter-cut. This makes them appear on a collision course. But at the last minute they go single file through a turnstile. We are disappointed. Then seconds later our wish is granted. They do meet. Under a train table, one knocks the shoe of the other. Now we are nervous. Visually, their meeting has already implied collision. This makes us lean in all the more as we suspect, it is all going to be bad — *very bad*.

Dramatic Value

By using screen direction to graphically suggest a pending collision, the film has set up conflict and character, and peaked our fears — all in under sixty seconds.

Script Note

Director Alfred Hitchcock lengthened the scene written by Czensi Ormonde and Raymond Chandler by extending the intercutting.

Other Films

Kill Bill (direction of footsteps)
Dances with Wolves (protagonist rides in the opposite direction of the soldiers)

Strangers on a Train (1951)

Screenplay: Czenzi Ormonde, Raymond Chandler.

```
FADE IN:

EXT. UNION STATION, WASHINGTON, D.C. DAY

LONG SHOT THE CAPITOL DOME IN THE B.G. AND THE AUTOMOBILE ENTRANCE TO
THE STATION IN THE F.G. LOW CAMERA.
```

Activity of cars and taxis arriving and discharging passengers with luggage, busy redcaps, etcetera.

We FOCUS on a taxi pulling up and stopping, The driver hands out modest looking luggage, including a bunch of tennis rackets in cases to a redcap. CAMERA PANS DOWN as the passenger gets out of the taxi so that we see only his shoes and the lower part of his trousers. He is wearing dark colored brogues and a conservative suit apparently. The feet move toward, the entrance to the station and out of scene. Immediately a chauffeur-driven limousine drives up and an expensive piece of airplane luggage is handed out of this, and the passenger alighting from the back is seen to be wearing a black and white sports shoes which, as seen before, are all we see of him. The sport shoes start off in the wake of the brogues.

```
INT. STATION LOBBY
```

CAMERA FOLLOWS the sport shoes and the brogues across the lobby into a passenger tunnel. There is the usual activity of passengers walking to and from, a loud-speaker announcing trains, etc.

```
EXT. PASSENGER TUNNEL
```

As the brogues and the sport shoes pass separately down the aisle, the sport shoes turning in at a compartment door and the brogues continuing toward the parlor car.

```
DISSOLVE TO:

INT. PARLOR CAR (PROCESS)
```

The brogues come to rest before a chair as the owner sits down. A moment later the sport shoes come to rest before an adjoining chair.

The legs belonging to the sport shoes stretch out, and one of the shoes touches one of the brogues.

```
MAN'S VOICE (over scene)

Oh, excuse me!
```

2.

1.

3.

4.

5.

6.

2. Film Element: Y-Axis (Vertical)

As we said in the previous section, the Y-axis is the line that travels from top <--> bottom in the frame along the north-south axis.

When an object runs along an axis in a straight line, and moves at a fixed speed, we automatically assume that the "good" destination is somewhere along the trajectory. Staying on track is a deep-felt virtue. Detouring or being sidetracked has negative connotations. Children's fables are filled with mishaps that occur when characters venture away from established routes. Hitchcock translated these assumptions pictorially in *Strangers on a Train*. Once the protagonist and antagonist meet in their train compartment, Hitchcock immediately cuts outside to the trainyard. Here he uses graphics to foreshadow the bumpy road ahead.

Film Example: *Strangers on a Train*

After already graphically suggesting that the meeting of the men will result in collision, Hitchcock cuts to an exterior insert shot. Hitchcock takes us to the train tracks upon which their train is traveling. At first we see only clean linear lines of the track. The train is "on course." It moves smoothly with a fixed speed and an unobstructed route ahead. Now we come upon an exchange of tracks. The lines are a mess of competing directions. Then — suddenly the train veers off. It heads toward the right side of the frame. This is the same side previously occupied by the antagonist. The graphics suggest that the protagonist has abandoned his true course and moved to the world of the antagonist.

Dramatic Value

By using the Y-axis to set up a linear established route, one that represents safety and normalcy, Hitchcock could also establish its opposite — the dangerous detour. The metaphor is also a succinct synopsis of the plot: What happens to a good man when his path is suddenly diverted?

Script Note

The insert to the train tracks was not included in this version of the script. Instead the scene between the men in the train car continues with the two men chatting about their backgrounds for several more pages. In the final film, the insert gives visual rest from the talking heads and acts to foreshadow the road ahead.

3. Film Element: XY-Axes (Diagonals)

In addition to the X, Y, and Z axes, a frame also contains four diagonals.

Descending Diagonals
Gravity aids the motion of descending diagonals. The descent seems easy, possibly inevitable. Once the motion starts, it's hard to stop. The left-to-right is an easier descent as it moves in the direction of the reading eye.

Ascending Diagonals
Gravity works against the ascending diagonals. It is easier to fall downwards, then move upwards. The right-left ascent is the most difficult of all screen directions: It goes against the reading eye and works against gravity as well.

Film Examples: *Metropolis, The Piano*
Both shots on the right exploit the "inevitability of the descent."

Metropolis: Workers are seen robotically making their daily descent "beneath."

The Piano: In realizing his wife has betrayed him, Stewart, Ada's husband, rushes with axe in hand to punish her.

Dramatic Value
Because gravity aids the descent, we know that nothing but a major intervention could stop the course of events.

Metropolis and *The Piano* are like textbooks on the use of graphics. Both are phenomenal films worth multiple viewings.

Fig. 3
Difficulty of Movement

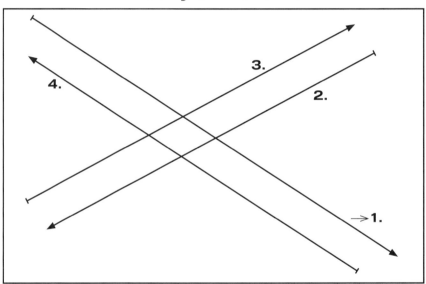

1. **Easiest**
2. **Less Easy**
3. **Hard**
4. **Hardest**

Metropolis

The Piano (1993) (Page 60)

Screenplay: Jane Campion, 4th Draft 1991.

```
Sc 117  EXT      STEWART'S    DAY
```
The sky is dark and rain is falling heavily as STEWART strides fast towards the hut, his axe swinging in his hand. FLORA is far behind him, her angelwings sodden.

The Piano

4. Film Element: Z-Axis (Depth-of-Field)

The Z-axis is the line that runs from foreground <--> background. It's what carries the illusion of depth. Technically, depth-of-field refers to the distance along the Z-axis that is in focus, or focal length. The wider the lens, the longer the focal length. Generally, a deep depth-of-field is achieved by two things: a wide-angle lens and lighting that will generate a higher f-stop.

The combination of a wide-angle lens and deep depth-of-field provides an intriguing visual characteristic: The distance an object moves along the Z-axis will appear foreshortened. For example, when characters move from the foreground to the background their height is diminished more quickly than expected. When they return to the foreground they seem to leap towards the camera, becoming larger, faster than the eye expects. The reverse is true with a telephoto lens.

The success of the following scene relies on two qualities:
a) the inherent foreshortening quality of the wide-angle lens and
b) the extended depth-of-field that keeps objects in the foreground and background in focus simultaneously.

Film Example: *Citizen Kane*

Though not included in the original screenplay, the scene between Kane, Thatcher and Bernstein is one of the single most ingenious scenes in cinema history. Here's the setup.

Kane has just learned from his guardian, Thatcher, that the Crash of '29 has wiped out his estate. Kane, a grown man, has been returned to the state of boyhood. Once again he is dependent on his guardian.

On hearing that he will be put on an allowance, Kane walks into the foreground of the frame, a huge, massive figure. He then travels down the Z-axis towards the back wall of the large room. Each step makes him appear smaller. He reaches the back wall and turns. He is about half the man he was a moment ago. Then Kane walks back toward Thatcher. With each step he regains some of his former stature. When he now stands beside Thatcher, once again appearing "full size," Thatcher suggests that the economic problems are just temporary. Without a word of dialog from Kane, Orson Welles has communicated Kane's inner turmoil.

Dramatic Value

Depth-of-field can
a) change a character's size as they move within the frame and
b) represent a character's size relative to other characters within the frame.

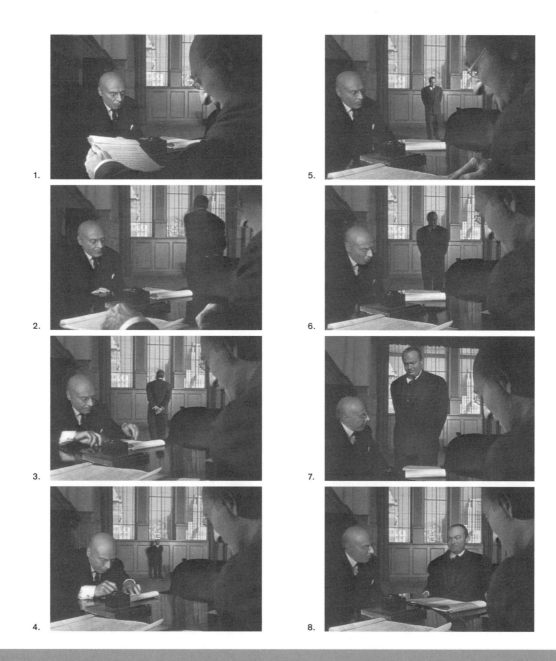

1.

2.

3.

4.

5.

6.

7.

8.

5. Film Element: Z-Axis (Planes of Action)

Painters divide the static frame into three planes. These are *foreground*, *middleground*, and *background*. For the filmmaker these zones can be used to stage different story elements.

Theatre has long used upstage, middlestage, and downstage as separate time zones or locations. A character may be upstage in the present observing his past which plays behind him downstage. A masterful use of this principle can be seen in a flashback scene in *Dolores Claiborne*.

Film Example: *Dolores Claiborne*

In this scene, protagonist Dolores Claiborne realizes that her twenty-something daughter has no recollection of being sexually abused by her father. Dolores stands in the foreground; her daughter is seated at a table in the middleground. Dolores reacts to her discovery by looking over her daughter to the background where the front door is positioned. On her look, a flashback begins in the background *only*. Dolores' husband, now twenty years younger, enters. He moves around in the background in one time zone, that of twenty years ago, while Dolores and her daughter are situated in the foreground and middleground, in another. As Dolores' daughter continues debating with her mother in the present, Dolores watches her dead husband causally walk behind her daughter into another room — and into a full flashback.

Dramatic Value

By exploiting the three planes of action, the past and the present can play alongside each other. Staging can help further externalize the subtext of the script. In this scene, for example, Dolores faces the past straight on while her daughter has her back to it.

Other Films

Citizen Kane (Susan's overdose scene)
Citizen Kane (snowball scene)

Dolores Claiborne (1995) (Pages 29-30)

Screenplay: Tony Gilroy, Third Draft 3/11/94.
Based on the novel by Stephen King.

Dolores silently clearing the table, when her eyes move past SELENA
suddenly, toward the door and --

DOLORES'S POV -- FLASHBACK

   The front door will open. The bright base of a summer sunset will
blow out the landscape beyond. This light will come only through the
door. The rest of the house -- still in the "present" -- will remain
dark.

   JOE ST. GEORGE will enter the house. He is thirty-five. A scrappy
build. A bad haircut. He is coming home from work. He's thirsty and
dirty. Standing in the doorway unlacing his boots.

(Note: Selena has no idea what her mother is seeing beyond her.
Dolores will continue to relate to Selena as if this were not
happening, trying to ignore this "presence" as the scene progresses.)

                    SELENA
           Look, let's face it mother --
           we barely know each other.
           We've hardly spoken in years.
           And that's as much your doing as mine.

Joe in stocking feet, banging the mud from his boots in the doorway.

(Selena continues talking while Dolores stares at the image of Joe
from the past in the background--- the scene continues briefly then
into a ---

FULL FLASHBACK

THE HOUSE. Suddenly full of light. The décor different. We are in
the Summer of 1972. SELENA, hearing her father rushes out from the
kitchen. She is nine. A gorgeous child.

6. Film Element: Z-Axis (Rack Focus)

A *Rack Focus* shot, also called a Pull Focus, requires a shallow depth-of-field. This means that only a narrow plane along the Z-axis can be in focus at one time. When the camera operator "pulls focus" he/she shifts the focus from one focal plane to another. In so doing, the audience's attention shifts from objects situated on one plane to objects on another. By creating a shallow depth-of-field, the in-camera effect can selectively redirect the audience's attention anytime during the scene. Here's how it was used in *The Graduate* in a pivotal scene at the end of Act Two.

Film Example: *The Graduate*

Ben, the twenty-something protagonist, has just returned home from college. On his return he has an affair with one of his parents' friends, Mrs. Robinson. The problem is that Ben soon falls in love with Mrs. Robinson's daughter, Elaine.

At the end of Act Two, Ben rushes to confess to Elaine. He breaks into her parents' home and finds Elaine in her upstairs bedroom. Before he can tell her, Mrs. Robinson's approaching footsteps can be heard. Elaine faces Ben with her back to the open bedroom door behind her. As Ben starts to explain why the identity of the older woman is important, Elaine's mother appears at the door.

Unseen by Elaine, who is still facing Ben, Mrs. Robinson stands in the doorway. Mrs. Robinson is out-of focus and ghost-like. When Elaine spins around, Mrs. Robinson is pulled into focus and Elaine is thrown out of focus. Every line in Mrs. Robinson's defeated face now shows. After a beat, Mrs. Robinson disappears from the door. When Elaine turns back to Ben, her face remains momentarily blurred externalizing her confusion. At the moment of recognition, her face is pulled back into focus.

In this scene, pull-focus does two things:
a) Reveals identity, in this case, that of the "older woman," Mrs. Robinson. Mrs. Robinson physically answers Elaine's unanswered question by suddenly being pulled into focus.
b) Externalizes Elaine's confusion by waiting for her moment of recognition to pull her back into focus.

Dramatic Value

Rack focus allows you to redirect the audience's attention from one object to another. It is often used to effect surprise through a sudden reveal, usually an important plot point. Since it heavily underscores the reveal, it should be used sparingly.

Other Films

Last Tango in Paris
The Professional (Leon's dying scene)

Historical Note

D.W. Griffith experimented with "rack focus" in the opening shot of *A Corner of Wheat* (1909), as well as *Musketeers of Pig Valley* (1912) and *The House of Darkness* (1913) (Jesionowski 35).

The Graduate (1967)

Screenplay: Calder Willingham and Buck Henry, 1967.
Novel: Charles Webb.

```
INT. ELAINE'S ROOM-DAY
```

Ben pulls ELAINE around behind the open door. They stand in the
angle formed by the door and the wall as though they were hiding from
someone. MRS. ROBINSON'S footsteps can be heard coming up the stairs.

```
                    BEN
        Elaine--I have to tell you something.
```

He holds her against the wall in the corner.

```
                    ELAINE
        What is it?
                    BEN
        That woman--
                    ELAINE
        What?
                    BEN
        That woman. The older woman.
                    ELAINE
        You mean the one who--
                    BEN
        The married woman--it wasn't just *some woman*--
                    ELAINE
        What are you telling me?
```

The footsteps stop.

```
ANGLE - CLOSE ON ELAINE
```

Back in the corner. Mrs. Robinson's face appears in a crack in the
door at Elaine's shoulder. Elaine looks from Ben's face to the crack
through which she can see her mother's eye staring.

```
                    ELAINE
        Benjamin, will you please tell me what this is all about.
```

She looks back at Ben, then back at her mother's face again. Mrs.
Robinson's eyes watch her through the crack in the door. Elaine looks
away.

```
                    ELAINE
        Oh no.
```

Chapter Credits By Film Element

1. *Strangers on a Train* (1951)
Writers: Czenzi Ormonde, Raymond Chandler (Screenplay)
Writer: Whitfield Cook (Adaptation)
Writer: Patricia Highsmith (Novel)
Director: Alfred Hitchcock
Production Company: Warner Brothers
Distributor: Warner Brothers

2. *Strangers on a Train* (1951)
Same as above.

3. *Metropolis* (1927)
Writer: Thea von Harbou (Screenplay)
Writer: Thea von Harbou (Novel)
Director: Fritz Lang
Production Company: Universum Film A.G. (UFA)
Distributor: Kino International

3. *The Piano* (1993)
Writer: Jane Campion
Director: Jane Campion
Production Company: Australian Film Commission, CiBy, New South Wales Film and Television Office
Distributor: Miramax Films

4. *Citizen Kane* (1941)
Writer: Herman J. Mankiewicz (Screenplay) and
Writer: Orson Welles (Screenplay)
Writer: John Houseman (Screenplay) (Uncredited)
Director: Orson Welles
Production Company: Mercury Productions
Production Company: RKO Pictures
Distributor: RKO Pictures Inc. (1941) USA Theatrical
Distributor: Warner Home Video (DVD)

5. *Dolores Claiborne* (1995)
Writer: Tony Gilroy (Screenplay)
Writer: Stephen King (Novel)
Director: Taylor Hackford
Production Company: Castle Rock Entertainment
Production Company: Columbia Pictures Corporation
Distributor: Columbia Pictures

6. *The Graduate* (1967)
Writer: Calder Willingham (Screenplay) and
Writer: Buck Henry (Screenplay)
Writer: Charles Webb (Novel)
Director: Mike Nichols
Production Company: Embassy Pictures
Production Company: Lawrence Turman Inc.
Distributor: MGM Home Entertainment (DVD)

SECTION 2

FRAME

FRAME: COMPOSITION

Since the beginning of film, theorists like Lev Kuleshov have tried to understand how the eye responds to visual stimuli.

Among the most important elements that have been discerned are: brightness, color, size, shape, motion, speed, and direction. Through careful manipulation, these elements can guide the audience's attention and emotional response. As always, content, juxtaposition with bordering frames, and the intersection of other elements will contribute to the viewer's response.

Suggested Reading

1. Kuleshov, Lev. *Kuleshov on Film 1922–1968*. Translated and edited with an introduction by Ronald Levaco, Berkeley: University of California Press, 1974.

2. Arnheim, Rudolph. *Art and Visual Perception*. Berkeley: University of California Press, 1954.

3. ———. *Visual Thinking*. Berkeley: University of California Press, 1969.

4. Lumet, Sidney. *Making Movies*. New York: Alfred A Knopf, 1995.

Film Elements

7. Directing the Eye	*Citizen Kane*	(journalists)
8. Imbalance	*Disco Pigs*	(incubator)
9. Balance	*Disco Pigs*	(teenagers)
10. Orientation	*Apocalypse Now* *Bound*	(upside-down face) (money)
11. Size	*Metropolis*	(contrasting images)

7. Film Element: Directing the Eye

In the following example from *Citizen Kane,* light and dark function as visual signposts. What's important is lit, what's unimportant is left in darkness.

Film Example: *Citizen Kane*

The journalist scene in *Citizen Kane* sets up the central question of the movie. Here we see a number of journalists watching the last frames of a newsreel depicting Kane's life.

We expect that when the newsreel is over, the empty screen would be unimportant and the journalists, who now take over the scene, would be central. However, the opposite is shown. The journalists are left in darkness and the blank white screen remains illuminated.

The inversion cues the audience that it is the *riddle* that is important, not the individual journalists who seek its answer. By de-emphasizing the visuals, the audience is also subconsciously directed to pay closer attention to the dialog. The importance of the dialog is further underscored by repetition. The state of journalists' knowledge is represented by the blank screen. This tells the audience that we are at the beginning of the quest and, by the end of the movie, the screen will contain the answer.

Dramatic Value

Light and dark are used as signposts. From their directives, the audience knows what to focus on.

Script Note

Note how fully the writer employs light as a dramatic tool. Despite minor alterations in the final film, the scene was largely shot as written.

Citizen Kane (1941)

Screenplay: Herman J. Mankiewicz and Orson Welles.

INT. PROJECTION ROOM - DAY

A fairly large one, with a long throw to the screen. It is dark.

The image of Kane as an old man remains constant on the screen as camera pulls back, slowly taking in and registering Projection Room. This action occurs, however, only after the first few lines of ensuing dialog have been spoken. The shadows of the men speaking appear as they rise from their chairs - black against the image of Kane' face on the screen.

Note: These are the editors of a "News Digest" short, and of the Rawlston magazines. All his enterprises are represented in the projection room, and Rawlston himself, the great man, is present also and will shortly speak up.

During the entire course of this scene, nobody's face is really seen. Sections of their bodies are picked out by a table light, a silhouette is thrown on the screen, and their faces and bodies are themselves thrown into silhouette against the brilliant slanting rays of light from the projection room.

A Third Man is on the telephone. We see a corner of his head and the phone.

                  THIRD MAN
                  (at phone)
        Stand by. I'll tell you if you want to run it again.

                  (hangs up)

                  THOMPSON'S VOICE
        Well?

A short pause.

                  A MAN'S VOICE
        It's a tough thing to do in a newsreel. Seventy years of a man's life -

Murmur of highly salaried assent at this. Rawlston walks toward camera and out of picture. Others are rising. Camera during all of this, apparently does its best to follow action and pick up faces, but fails. Actually, all set-ups are to be planned very carefully to exclude the element of personality from this scene; which is expressed entirely by voices, shadows, silhouettes and the big, bright image of Kane himself on the screen.

1.

2.

3.

4.

5.

6.

7.

8.

8. Film Element: Imbalance

A balanced frame is one in which there is an intentional symmetry. Mass, color, size, shape, complexity, and implied direction are manipulated to create this effect. In the brilliant independent film, *Disco Pigs*, written by Enda Walsh and based on his play of the same name, balance and imbalance are ingeniously exploited. The script example is taken from the second scene of this coming-of-age film set in Ireland and beautifully directed by Kirsten Sheridan.

Film Example: *Disco Pigs*

The movie opens with a baby in-utero fighting her way through the punishing birth canal. The baby's voiceover makes it clear that she's not liking it. Then we cut to an incubator where the newborn now lies calmly.

The next scene starts with a high-angle shot of what first appears to be a perfectly balanced shot: We see two identical cribs positioned side by side. What sabotages the balance is that only one of the cribs is occupied. The emptiness of the crib is underscored by the otherwise perfect symmetry. It also externalizes the newborn's dilemma — her loneliness for a playmate.

Then she hears a howl. A baby boy now lies in the formerly empty crib. After the two newborns exchange glances, we cut to a high-angle shot identical to the first. This time both cribs are occupied. The imbalance of the first shot has been remedied. We then cut to the babies reaching out to each other in an equally symmetric frame.

Both problem and solution are externalized by this clever use of graphics.

Dramatic Value

By using balance and imbalance, the writer and director have established the initial conflict in the script. Later it is the symbiotic relationship that at first appeared as a solution, that becomes the central conflict in the film.

Other Films

Hedwig and the Angry Inch

Disco Pigs (2001)

Screenplay: Enda Walsh, based on the play: Enda Walsh.

```
INT. HOSPITAL WARD - DAY
```

The baby RUNT in a cot looking up at the bright light white tiled ceiling.

We can hear the muffled sounds of people chatting and walking back and forth.

> RUNT V/O
> Only a few months old and I start thinkin things even then.
> Starin' at that white sky right above me, and I want for something
> altogether different.

We hear the cries of another baby.

RUNT'S point of view searches it out.

> RUNT V/O
> And that's when I hear him again. For out he bounce inta the whirl
> of grey happiness just like me. Same time even we take our furs
> bread. Like magic.

We see a mural wall of Toytown.

> RUNT V/O
> And through the Noddy and Big Ears wall I search after his cry. The
> cry so lonely it scares and makes me cry too.

We watch from above the two cots with the baby RUNT and baby PIG both screaming
crying.

They are slowly turning into each other.

> RUNT V/O
> And all the sights that we could see they go invisible when we hear
> each other's cries. And that's when the magic it all begin. It begin
> when the baby-Pig and baby-Runt stare through her baby eyes, ya
> see. And the cryin and screamin it stop. And that's when I feel him
> close. We join, me and him. Pig look right inta me and I see myself
> when I look back inta his baby eyes. I calm the crying down then.
> From that moment we become one. And we need no one else. No body.

The two babies have reached out over the space between the cots.

> RUNT V/O
> The King and Queen, settle and calm in a colour not of grey, but
> something good and new.

Magically their arms have stretched out to each other and eventually join.

The babies laugh.

> RUNT V/O
> A colour of their own makin'…

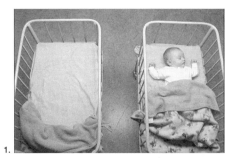
1.

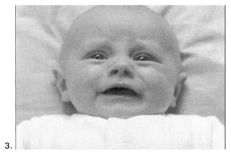
2.

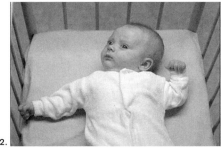
3.

4.

9. Film Element: Balance

See above.

Film Example: *Disco Pigs*

We now move to the third scene in the movie. Here we again meet the newborns, who are now teenagers. The opening shot perfectly mimics the symmetry of the previous scene. Once again, the frame is perfectly balanced. The boy takes up the left side of the shot and the girl, the right. The couple is still holding hands. The pointed visual cues make us confident that the teenagers are the newborns from the previous scene.

Through the use of graphics, the scene suggests that the symbiotic relationship, established in the hospital incubator, has continued uninterrupted for the past fifteen years. The idea is conveyed largely by graphic principles.

Dramatic Value

By coding characters early in a film, their symbols can be recalled later. In this instance the teenagers are immediately identified without exposition despite a lengthy passage of time.

Other Films

The Graduate (two-shot of couple, last scene, riding in the back of the bus.)

Disco Pigs (2001)

Screenplay: Enda Walsh, based on the play: Enda Walsh.

```
EXT. PIG AND RUNT'S HOUSES - NIGHT
```

PIG and RUNT stop outside their terraced houses which stand side by side.

They are small grey houses with small gardens in front.

They stand looking at them.

The exterior of RUNT'S house is slightly shabbier than the exterior of PIG's.

They turn to each other.

```
                    PIG
          Night so, sweet thing.
                    RUNT
          Cheerio, ol pal.
          PIG
          Don't let the bed bugs bite, hah?
                    RUNT
          I'll bite the fuckers back!
```

PIG laughs.

```
                    PIG
          Tomorrow so?
                    RUNT
                    (she smiles)
          What else!!
                    PIG
          Night, beautiful.
                    RUNT
          Night night.
```

They both open up the gates into their houses and walk towards their doors.

They stop and both knock on the doors loudly.

Both doors are opened at the same time.

We hear the shouting of annoyed parents.

1.

2.

3.

10. Film Element: Orientation

As audiences, we expect the composition to make viewership simple. We expect that the movie world will come with enhancements, but essentially present the world intact. When the basic rules of viewer orientation are broken, they draw attention to themselves. Consequently when they are used, they need to mean something — or they'll be rejected.

Introducing a character upside-down, for example, clearly breaks the rules. We are so unaccustomed to this vantage point, we will move our heads trying to correct it. Seeing an extreme close-up, such as an ear or eye, is similarly disorienting. However, when purposefully used, disorientation can be highly effective.

In both *Apocalypse Now* and *Barton Fink*, the protagonists are turned upside-down. Yet the shots are beautifully integrated into the scenes and serve to advance their story.

Film Examples: *Apocalypse Now, Barton Fink*

Apocalypse Now: In the opening shots of *Apocalypse Now* we see the jungle of Vietnam burning. Between a series of dissolves the face of Captain Willard, a young American soldier, emerges. His face is upside-down. This cautions the audience that the story we are about to hear isn't going to be ordinary. It also tells us that Willard is not going to be ordinary.

Barton Fink: Like Captain Willard, Barton is a man who is not at home. Forced by his agent to cash in on his success as a Broadway playwright, Barton reluctantly leaves his artistic cocoon for Hollywood. As Barton lies in bed in his L.A. hotel room, the camera begins to rotate. The drifting bed and the inverted orientation are metaphors for his inner turmoil. Later in the movie, Barton will find a dead woman in the same bed, making the shot feel like a premonition.

Dramatic Value

A disorienting shot intentionally disorients. If done carefully, it can externalize a character's inner world or even, as in the case of *Barton Fink*, be prescient. Disorientation is effective because we expect to see the world from a familiar perspective; any detour from that view will dramatically underscore a scene.

Other Films

The Lodger (1927) (low angle of a lodger pacing above, shot through a glass floor)

The Professional (POV scene where Leon falls after being shot, dying scene)

Jaws, Bound, Eraserhead, Metropolis

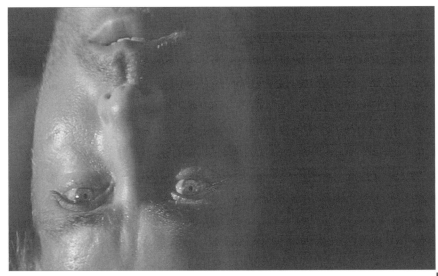

Apocalypse Now

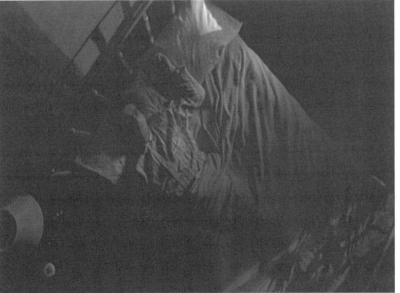

Barton Fink

11. Film Element: Size

A character's relative strength and weakness can be established by the use of size.

Film Example: *Metropolis*

In Fritz Lang's brilliant film *Metropolis* (1927) he depicts two worlds:

Shot 1

The outer world is the world of soaring modern buildings that represent the best of man's technical achievement. These mammoth architectural feats dominate the frame and seemingly stretch up to the clouds. Only the elite in this metropolis live above ground to enjoy its benefits.

Shot 2

Lang contrasts the massive skyscrapers with the ant-like men who build them. These dehumanized workers shuffle along in columns and are forced to live in "ant colonies," beneath the ground. The workers are dwarfed by the building they create and the machines that enslave them.

Dramatic Value

Lang uses size to contrast the power of the "upper world" with the "world beneath."

Other Films

Citizen Kane (fireplace scene: Kane versus Susan)

ET (introduction: trucks versus ET)

Jaws (throughout the movie: sharks versus man)

1.

2.

Chapter Credits By Film Element

7. *Citizen Kane* (1941)

Writer:	Herman J. Mankiewicz (Screenplay) and
Writer:	Orson Welles (Screenplay)
Writer:	John Houseman (Screenplay) (Uncredited)
Director:	Orson Welles
Production Company:	Mercury Productions
Production Company:	RKO Pictures
Distributor:	RKO Pictures Inc. (1941) USA Theatrical
Distributor:	Warner Home Video (DVD)

8. *Disco Pigs* (2001)

Writer:	Enda Walsh
Writer:	Enda Walsh
Director:	Kirsten Sheridan
Production Company:	Temple Film & TV Productions Ltd
Distributor:	Renaissance Films

9. *Disco Pigs* (2001)
Same as above.

10. *Apocalypse Now* (1979)

Writer:	John Milius (Screenplay) and
Writer:	Francis Coppola (Screenplay)
Writer:	Joseph Conrad (Uncredited)
Director:	Francis Coppola
Production Company:	Zoetrope
Distributor:	United Artists

11. *Metropolis* (1927)

Writer:	Thea von Harbou (Screenplay)
Writer:	Thea von Harbou (Novel)
Director:	Fritz Lang
Production Company:	Universum Film A.G. (UFA)
Distributor:	Kino International

SECTION **3**

SHAPE
WITHIN THE
FRAME

SHAPE WITHIN THE FRAME

Depending on use and context, shapes can be used to suggest ideas and a range of emotions. Traditionally we accept that there are three fundamental shapes:

The circle

The square

The triangle

From these many other forms derive: The half-circle, the rectangle, the heart, the octagon, and so on, as well as a limitless number of organic forms.

Traditional Associations
Visual theorists often link shapes with specific emotions or ideas. Here's the list from Bruce Block's book *The Visual Story*, a superb guide to exploiting visual principles for the screen.

Rounded shapes
"Indirect, passive, romantic, pertaining to nature, soft organic, childlike, safe and flexible."

Square shapes
"Direct, industrial, ordered, linear, unnatural, adult, and rigid."

Triangles
"Aggressive and dynamic" (Block 86).

Block cautions, however, that these are not rules. New associations can always be made depending on the needs of the story. Shape is also just one element in the frame.

In Robert Altman's *Three Women*, shape was trumped by color. The protagonist handled a variety of shaped props that were predominately pink in Act One. When the character changed, "her color" changed. Color, not shape, was chosen as the primary visual messenger. Alternatively, shape was pointedly used in *Witness*, where the triangle was used to suggest the dynamic of a lover's triangle.

Storytelling

A writer or director can use shape to create a dynamic location within a scene. This might be a one-time association or incorporated throughout the film. Characters can also be given competing signature shapes creating a visual conflict. Conversely, they can be given like shapes suggesting similarity. One of the most intriguing uses of shape is seen in Francis Coppola's *The Conversation* where the protagonist is linked with two shapes, one to suggest his outer persona, the other to suggest his inner persona.

Once characters are "coded," their change can be mapped by the audience over time.

Film Elements

12. Circular   *The Conversation* (conspiracy-location-tapes)

13. Linear   *Fargo* (tire tracks as crossroads)

14. Triangular   *Witness* (lover's triangle)

15. Rectangular   *The Searchers* (rectangle as portal)

16. Organic versus Geometric   *Witness*

12. Film Element: Circular

Whenever a symbol like light is used, it is far more effective when it's contrasted with its opposite. Similarly, the use of the circular is greatly augmented when its opposite, the linear, plays alongside. Circular imagery can inherently suggest confusion, repetition, and time, but it can also generate less obvious shadings when used with contrasting elements.

Film Example: *The Conversation*

According to writer-director Francis Coppola, *The Conversation* grew out of Coppola's interest in repetition (Coppola). In the script, Coppola symbolizes it with the circular. What is being repeated is man's emotional weakness represented by deceit and betrayal.

Coppola's protagonist, Harry (Gene Hackman), is a surveillance expert. His outer person is symbolized by the linear. He is rational, technically competent, detached, and remote. Coppola gives him clothes and a physical environment made up of straight, elongated lines.

Harry's job is dependent on the circular spinning wheels of the tape recorder. As long as he stays detached from their content, he is competent and stable.

However, when Harry gets uncharacteristically drawn into the emotional lives he records, he begins to spin out of control. Suddenly the disparity between his outer and inner competencies becomes clear. Harry cannot navigate the emotional world. His attempt becomes his undoing.

The plot has a beautiful circular quality. By the end of the movie, the surveillance expert becomes the surveillance subject. Harry completely disassembles his apartment in the final shots of the movie. The theme "what goes around, comes around" repeats the circularity of the plot and physical metaphors.

The scripted excerpt that follows, occurs when the protagonist tries to change the course of events. He enters a building that is linear on the outside, but circular on the inside — just like Harry. Once inside, he is confronted on the circular stairwell by corporate thugs. Below him is a floor tiled in a circular pattern. Once ejected from the building, he is safe again. He walks along the linear structure almost disappearing into its gray lined walls.

Dramatic Value

Characters can be given conflicting graphic symbols, in this case an outer and inner symbol. Once established they open up the story to "picture-telling." The audience can then actively participate in decoding the images, making the interpretation their own. Less reliance on dialog is necessary.

Other Films

Witness

The Conversation (1974)

Screenplay: Francis Coppola. Final Draft 11/22/72.

Note: Throughout the movie Harry walks in straight lines. The couple he tapes, Mark and Ann, moves in circles. They, like the other characters in the "film's conspiracy," are identified with the circle. Here are some selected excerpts that show how the circular and linear were played off each other.

24. EXT. WAREHOUSE AREA DAY (page 24)

Harry walks parallel to some railroad tracks in the industrial part of the city.

161 EXT. UNION SQUARE DAY

Mark and Ann in their perpetual walk around Union Square.

174 HIGH ANGLE

The intersection, normally crowded with people and cars, now totally bare, accented by the white road markings and bus stops. Harry Caul crosses the intersection and makes his way to the patterned sidewalk which designates the Financial building plaza.

178 INT THE LOBBY - DAY

The bell clinks. Harry steps out into the main lobby. No one sits at the receptionist desk.

He proceeds to the desk, and up the spiral staircase.

179 INT THE MAZE DAY

Harry enters; the once busy maze is now totally empty.

201 EXT THE FINANCIAL DISTRICT DAY

Bleak and desolate.

Harry walks along the plaza alone.

202 MOVING VIEW ON HARRY

As he walks, he seems to be in an emotional quandary, raging over the role he has played in this. He walks blindly in a straight line.

1.

2.

3.

4.

13. Film Element: Linear

Linear simply refers to the use of lines. Lines can externalize any number of abstract ideas. When made physical, they offer another way of communicating ideas. In the example below, Jerry Lundegard, the protagonist in the Coen Brothers' *Fargo*, is at a "crossroads." The Coen brothers physically express this idea by carving out a set of "crossroads" into the snow through the use of snow tires. Here's more about the scene.

Film Example: *Fargo*

Fargo's protagonist, Jerry Lundegard, is a bumbling car salesman who is over his head in debt. He decides to have his rich wife kidnapped. The plan is dependent on his father-in-law paying the ransom. Jerry will act as the middle-man, pocket the ransom, then pay off his debts. At the last minute, he has a chance to make the money another way. But his father-in-law thwarts the deal. Jerry is now at a crossroads. Jerry can confess his responsibility for the kidnapping that is already in motion, or see it to the end.

The Coen brothers beautifully externalize Jerry's "crossroads" moment. The scene opens with a high-angle shot of a snow-covered parking lot. There is a huge "cross" in the frame made by snow tires. Jerry approaches the "crossroads." Instead of returning to his father-in-law's office and confessing what he's done, he advances past the crossroads and gets into his parked car. Once inside he realizes he isn't going to stop the plan. He jumps out, and hacks away at the ice-covered windshield with a scraper. He knows he's weak, and hates himself for it.

Dramatic Value

Symbolic use of graphics can externalize ideas and character choices. If set up properly they can also help us measure a character's decision-making over time. For example, if symbols of success are put up on the screen, then the audience can judge how close characters are in attaining them, or how far they still have to go.

Script Note

In this version of the script, the first half of the scene only mentions the high-angle. The rest of the scripted scene focuses on Jerry's scraping of the windshield. In the filmed version the first half of the scene is expanded and introduces a crossroads metaphor which greatly enhances the actions that follow.

Other Films

Witness

Metropolis

Fargo (1996)

Screenplay: Joel Coen & Ethan Coen, Draft: Nov. 2, 1994.

PARKING LOT

We are high and wide on the office building's parking lot.

Jerry emerges wrapped in a parka, his arms sticking stiffly out at his sides, his breath vaporizing. He goes to his car, opens its front door, pulls out a red plastic scraper and starts methodically scraping off the thin crust of ice that has developed on his windshield.

The scrape-scrape-scrape sound carries in the frigid air.

Jerry goes into a frenzy, banging the scraper against the windshield and the hood of his car.

The tantrum passes. Jerry stands panting, staring at nothing in particular.

Scrape-scrape-scrape - he goes back to work on the windshield.

1.

3.

2.

14. Film Element: Triangular

A triangular element can be created by many devices such as: lighting, furnishings, exterior graphics, character positioning, or movement. A triangle might refer to the harmony of the family as in father, mother, and child. It might similarly conjure up a harmonious religious triad such as the Father, Son and Holy Ghost. However, the opposite can be inferred — that of disharmony — the unwanted third wheel in a friendship, or the conflict implied by a lover's triangle. The rational and mathematical can also be suggested. As always, the meaning of the symbol depends on rendering.

In the example below, taken from *Witness*, the triangular is put to classic use in expressing a lover's triangle. It is physically realized through character positioning and triangular graphics.

Film Example: *Witness*

After being shot trying to protect a young boy's life, John Book, a Philadelphia cop, finds himself living in an Amish community.

While convalescing, Book has fallen in love with Rachel, a recently widowed Amish woman. However, before Book arrived, Rachel had been romantically pursued by a member of her community, Hochstetler. (His name was changed in the film.)

Rachel's conflict is visually represented by physically positioning the characters in a "lover's triangle." Rachel and her Amish caller are seated on either side of a bench located on the front porch. Book looks on from the lawn. They are surrounded by other triangular images: the birdhouse, the area behind Book, the pitched roof of the barn, the pathway forming three triangles, the top of the porch beams, and the branches of the trees.

Script Note

Notice how the scriptwriters create a triangle by the character's positioning. This is true in both scenes that play back to back in the scripted pages that follow. In the final film these two scenes were collapsed into one and the location was slightly altered, but the triangular positioning was retained.

Dramatic Value

The graphics express the lover's triangle the three are caught in. When new shapes appear, we know that a change has occurred.

Witness (1985)

Screenplay: William Kelley, Earl Wallace, Revised Draft, April 23, 1984

Scene Setup: Hochstetler, Rachel's Amish suitor, approaches Rachel's house. Hochstetler passes Book. Hochstetler claps Book on the shoulder and heads for the house.

93L ANGLE

As Rachel emerges from the house to greet him, she also catches sight of Book and pauses, a shadow of confusion crossing her expression for an instant.

And Hochstetler doesn't miss it either.

93M HOG PENS

Book, having gathered the pieces of the bird house, is headed toward the outbuildings, passing by hogpens.

He glances toward the house:

93N HIS POV - THE BACK PORCH

Where Rachel and Hochstetler are sitting in a porch swing, sharing a pitcher of lemonade.

93O BACK TO BOOK

Thoughtful... He glances at the hog pen as a huge sow squeals angrily noses her young ones away from the trough so she can feed.

                    BOOK
          Pigs.

1.

2.

3.

15. Film Element: Rectangular

Film Example: *The Searchers*

The Searchers (1956), written by Frank Nugent and directed by John Ford, remains one of the most admired westerns ever made. The conflict is immediately established with the opening shot. Here we learn that Uncle Ethan, played by John Wayne, is a single man unable to settle down. By the end of the film we realize that despite outward appearances, family values are not lost on him. Quite the contrary. In order to be strong enough to defend family values on the brutal Texas frontier of 1868, he has to remain an outsider. Here's how the opening shot elegantly expressed the theme of the movie.

The camera is placed inside a homesteader's home. The front door opens. It forms a huge bright rectangle that looks out to the blue sky of the untamed frontier. A woman is silhouetted in the door frame. Then we cut to what she sees. A man rides up, who will be identified as Uncle Ethan. He is like the untamed frontier. He blends into the organic shapes and colors of the landscape. The rectangular door is used throughout the film as the portal between the two worlds. The rectangular and flat interior shots are used to refer to domesticity; the organic shapes and deep-focus shots, to man's untamed self.

The last shot of the movie repeats the first. Now we understand that it is precisely because Uncle Ethan respects family values, that he cannot remain inside. He stands in the doorway looking in at the happy domestic scene. Despite the emotional draw, he finally turns and heads back out.

Dramatic Value

The rectangular is used to represent a portal to another world. It symbolizes the character's conflict and helps to externalize his choices.

Other Films

The Sweet Hereafter (see Film Element 95)

The Piano (rectangular piano as coffin, see Act 3)

The Searchers (1956) (Page 2)

Screenplay: Frank Nugent, Revised Final Draft.

Novel: Alan Le May.

```
EXT. THE EDWARDS HOUSE - MED. SHOT - AARON - LATE AFTERNOON
```

The ranch house is of adobe, solidly built, with a sod and cross-timbered roof, deep windows. A small gallery or porch extends across the front. AARON EDWARDS comes through the door, attracted by the dog's barking -- and then he, too, sees the approaching horseman and comes further out.

1.

2.

3.

4.

16. Film Element: Organic versus Geometric

In general, organic shapes are associated with nature, geometric shapes with man. These symbols can be used for different purposes. In *Witness* they distinguish the Amish from the urban; in *Metropolis*, they differentiate the oppressed from the oppressors.

Film Example: *Witness*

Protagonist John Book represents the American urban life. The Amish, with whom he comes to live, have rejected technology and urban commerce. They live simply and off the land.

Book's world is symbolized by geometric shapes, lines, squares, and rectangles.

The Amish, on the other hand, are represented by the circular, and naturally occurring forms like soft swaying stocks of wheat.

Film Example: *Metropolis* (not pictured)

Fritz Lang's *Metropolis* takes us into the future where an earthly high-tech utopia has been built. Its lines are linear and geometric.

Just outside the linear urban center, an elite paradise has been created for the few. Its lines are organic. Despite the initial appearance of beauty, it has an ugly underbelly, as it was built by those who are prohibited entry.

Dramatic Value

In *Witness* the contrast of shapes was used to underscore the central theme of the movie: that the two worlds (geometric and organic) could not easily mesh.

In *Metropolis*: The organic world is for the privileged only, a Garden of Eden for the few. It subverts the idea of the Garden's innocence as it is founded on brutal economic conditions. Here the organic has a negative meaning.

Take a look at how these graphic principles are used in the film excerpts on the accompanying page.

1.

2.

3.

3.

Chapter Credits By Film Element

12. *The Conversation* (1974)
Writer:	Francis Coppola
Director:	Francis Coppola
Production Company:	American Zoetrope
Production Company:	Paramount Pictures
Production Company:	The Coppola Company
Production Company:	The Directors Company
Distributor:	Paramount Pictures

13. *Fargo* (1996)
Writer:	Joel Coen (Screenplay) &
Writer:	Ethan Coen
Director:	Joel Coen
Director:	Ethan Coen (Uncredited)
Production Company:	Gramercy Pictures
Production Company:	Polygram Filmed Entertainment
Production Company:	Working Title Films
Distributor:	Concorde Home Entertainment (1998) (DVD)
Distributor:	Gramercy (USA) Theatrical

14. *Witness* (1985)
Writer:	William Kelley (Screenplay and Story)
Writer:	Earl Wallace (Screenplay and Story)
Writer:	Pam Wallace (Story)
Director:	Peter Weir
Production Company:	Paramount Pictures
Distributor:	Paramount Pictures

15. *The Searchers* (1956)
Writer:	Frank S. Nugent (Screenplay)
Writer:	Alan le May (Novel)
Director:	John Ford
Production Company:	C.V. Witney Pictures
Production Company:	Warner Bros.
Distributor:	Warner Bros.

16. *Witness* (1985)
Same as above.

SECTION **4**

EDITING

EDITING: PUDOVKIN'S FIVE EDITING TECHNIQUES

A Little Theory

Editing is the construction of scenes through the assembly of shots. In the 1920s when the great Russian theorists scoped out what the new elastic medium could do, they focused on the storytelling potential of editing.

Five Editing Principles

In the 1920s Vsevold Pudovkin set down five editing techniques that remain the foundation of modern day cutting. He named them as follows:

1. Contrast
2. Parallelism
3. Symbolism
4. Simultaneity
5. Leitmotif

For Pudovkin the purposeful use of editing could guide the audience's emotional response. Therefore he believed it was the job of both the writer and editor to master editing as their single most important job was the "psychological guidance" of the spectator." (Pudovkin 125)

Pudovkin's five principles show how editing choices can evoke specific audience emotions. As effective then as they are now, Pudovkin's principles are reproduced here as they appeared in *Film Theory and Criticism*, 4th edition (Eisenstein). Pudovkin first published his editing principles in his native Russian in 1926. Numbering was added for clarity.

Here's how Pudovkin explained his editing principles almost 100 years ago.

On Editing
—V. Pudovkin 1926

1. Contrast — Suppose it be our task to tell of the miserable situation of a starving man; the story will impress the more vividly if associated with mention of the senseless gluttony of a well-to-do man.

On just such a simple contrast relation is based the corresponding editing method. On the screen the impression of this contrast is yet increased, for it is possible not only to relate the starving sequence to the gluttony sequence, but also to relate separate scenes and even separate shots of scenes to one another, thus, as it were, forcing the spectator to compare the two actions all the time, one strengthening the other. The editing of contrast is one of the most effective, but also one of the commonest and most standardised, of methods, and so care should be taken not to overdo it.

2. Parallelism — This method resembles contrast, but is considerably wider. Its substance can be explained more clearly by an example. In a scenario as yet unproduced a section occurs as follows: a working man, one of the leaders of a strike, is condemned to death; the execution is fixed for 5 a.m. The sequence is edited thus: a factory-owner, employer of the condemned man, is leaving a restaurant drunk, he looks at his wrist-watch: 4 o'clock. The accused is shown — he is being made ready to be led out. Again the manufacturer, he rings a door-bell to ask the time: 4:30. The prison wagon drives along the street under heavy guard. The maid who opens the door — the wife of the condemned — is subjected to a sudden senseless assault. The drunken factory-owner snores on a bed, his leg with trouser-end upturned, his hand hanging down with wrist-watch visible, the hands of the watch crawl slowly to 5 o'clock. The workman is being hanged. In this instance two thematically unconnected incidents develop in parallel by means of the watch that tells of the approaching execution. The watch on the wrist of the callous brute, as it were connects him with the chief protagonist of the approaching tragic denouement, thus ever present in the consciousness of the spectator. This is undoubtedly an interesting method, capable of considerable development.

*3. **Symbolism** — In the final scenes of the film Strike the shooting down of workmen is punctuated by shots of the slaughter of a bull in the stockyard. The scenarist, as it were, desires to say: just as a butcher fells a bull with the swing of a pole-axe, so cruelly and in cold blood, were shot down the workers. This method is especially interesting because, by means of editing, it introduces an abstract concept into the consciousness of the spectator without use of a title.*

*4. **Simultaneity** — In American films the final section is constructed from the simultaneous rapid development of two actions, in which the outcome of one depends on the outcome of the other. The end of the present-day section of Intolerance… is thus constructed. The whole aim of this method is to create in the spectator a maximum tension of excitement by the constant forcing of a question, such as, in this case: Will they be in time? — will they be in time?*

The method is a purely emotional one, and nowadays overdone almost to the point of boredom, but it cannot be denied that of all the methods of constructing the end hitherto devised it is the most effective.

*5. **Leit-motif (reiteration of theme)** — Often it is interesting for the scenarist especially to emphasise the basic theme of the scenario. For this purpose exists the method of reiteration. Its nature can easily be demonstrated by an example. In an anti-religious scenario that aimed at exposing the cruelty and hypocrisy of the Church in employ of the Tsarist regime, the same shot was several times repeated: a church-bell slowly ringing and, superimposed on it, the title: "The sound of bells sends into the world a message of patience and love." This piece appeared whenever the scenarist desired to emphasise the stupidity of patience, or the hypocrisy of the love thus preached.*

—1926 (Pudovkin 125-6)

Further Reading

1. Pudovkin, Vsevolod. *Film Technique and Film Acting, 1926*. New York: Grove Press, 1970.
2. Eisenstein, Sergei. *Film Form: Essays in Film Theory*. Edited and translated by Jay Leyda. New York: Harcourt Brace & Co., 1949 (1977).
3. Kuleshov, Lev. *Kuleshov on Film, 1922-1968*. Selected, translated and edited with an introduction by Ronald Levaco. Berkeley: University of California Press, 1974.
4. Mast, Gerald, Marshall Cohen and Leo Brady, eds. *Film Theory and Criticism: Introductory Readings*. 4th Edition. London: Oxford University Press, 1992.

Editing: Additional Techniques

By the end of the 1920s the basics of scene construction had been laid down. Pudovkin along with Sergei Eisentein, D.W. Griffith, and Fritz Lang had so successfully advanced the craft that much of what followed were variations of their basic techniques.

In the same way that modern day editing is a footnote to these early pioneers, many of their inventions have been attributed to 19th century novelists. Eisenstein, for example, credited much of Griffith's early innovations like progressive montage, intercutting, the close-up and even the dissolve to the novels of Charles Dickens (Eisenstein 398). What these early theorists did was create film equivalents for proven literary forms while, at the same time, mining the new medium for yet undiscovered techniques.

Here is a representative selection of the staple editing techniques used by contemporary filmmakers.

Film Elements

17. Montage	*Citizen Kane*	22. Split Screen	*Kill Bill Vol. 1*
18. Montage	*Adaptation*	23. Dissolves	*Citizen Kane*
19. Assembly	*Psycho*	24. Dissolves	*Barton Fink*
20. Mise-en-scène	*Psycho*	25. Smash Cut	*American Beauty*
21. Intercutting	*Cabaret*		

17. Film Element: Montage

A *montage* is created through an assembly of quick cuts, disconnected in time or place, that combine to form a larger idea. A montage is frequently used to convey passage of time, coming of age, or emotional transition.

Originally "montage," which is a French term meaning "to assemble," referred to the creative construction of scenes from the "assembly of shots." Today it means a specific narrative construction — a series of shots usually without dialog.

Film Example: *Citizen Kane*

There are a number of superb montages in *Citizen Kane*. Interestingly, almost identically constructed montages are used to depict Kane's disintegrating relationship with both his first and second wife. Each montage takes place in a single setting, each shows the couple engaged in a single activity. The first shows the couple at the breakfast table. The second is set in a huge great room. Both montages return us to the same location and the same activity. There are no cutaways to other locations or characters. In this way the audience can focus on the changing behavior of the couple as the location and activity are unchanged. By showing the disintegration with a mirrored form, the montage is able to suggest a certain inevitability with respect to Kane's ability to hold onto relationships. It's as though the wives change, but the pattern of disintegration is constant. Here's a look at the second montage featuring Susan, Kane's second wife.

Susan's Montage

As we go into the montage, Kane and Susan are seen arguing as Susan works on a puzzle. When we come out of the montage, years later, the couple is still arguing and Susan is still working on a puzzle. In a brief two minutes of screen time, we get a sense of their prolonged unhappiness and its escalation over time.

The script uses the progression of puzzle-making to indicate the passage of time. The choice of puzzle-making as an activity also cleverly reminds us that Kane is as much an enigma to Susan as he is to the journalists. It's as though Kane himself is like an unending series of puzzles; as soon as one is done, another presents itself.

Dramatic Value

Here the montage suggests passage of time and character progression. By using the same construction twice, it allows the audience to make comparisons and, from that, new inferences.

Citizen Kane (1941)

Screenplay: Herman J. Mankiewicz and Orson Welles.

```
INT. THE GRAND HALL IN XANADU - 1925
```

Closeup of an enormous jigsaw puzzle. A hand is putting in the last piece. Camera moves back to reveal jigsaw puzzle spread out on the floor.

Susan is on the floor before her jigsaw puzzle. Kane is in an easy chair. Behind them towers the massive Renaissance fireplace. It is night and Baroque candelabra illuminates the scene.

(We are dropping in at the end of the scene)

```
                SUSAN
        If I promise to be a good girl!
        Not to drink - and to entertain
        all the governors and the senators
        with dignity -
        (she puts a slur into the word)
        Charlie -
```

There is still no answer.

```
DISSOLVE OUT:

DISSOLVE IN:
```

Another picture puzzle - Susan's hands fitting in a missing piece.

```
DISSOLVE:
```

Another picture puzzle - Susan's hands fitting in a missing piece.

```
DISSOLVE:

INT. XANADU - LIVING ROOM - DAY - 1928
```

Another picture puzzle.

Camera pulls back to show Kane and Susan in much the same positions as before, except that they are older.

1.

2.

3.

4.

18. Film Element: Montage

Character-driven movies often fail to enlist cinematic tools defaulting to dialog instead. The scripts appear more like "radio plays" or what Hitchcock has called "talking photographs." But there are many character-driven films like *The Piano*, *American Beauty*, and *Time of the Gypsies* that succeed beautifully. These films, like Charlie Kaufman's *Adaptation*, use the full complement of cinematic tools available.

Film Example: *Adaptation*

Charlie Kaufman's *Adaptation* opens on a black screen with a voiceover monologue, cuts to a scene establishing the character, and then returns to voice over which poses the questions "Why I am I here? How did I get here?" The question is met with a sweeping cinematic montage that immediately sets up tone and conflict. The montage takes us through the great evolutionary achievements of nature and of man. Finally we arrive at the last stage of evolutionary progression — Charlie Kaufman dining in an L.A. restaurant.

Dramatic Value

The montage gives the film a spectacular visual complement to the intelligence of the opening voice over and the introductory scene. It depicts the scope of the protagonist's historical and philosophical continuum and the impossible standard against which he will evaluate the meaning of his life. Right off the bat, we are given a clear picture of just how high the cards are stacked against the protagonist finding the answers he needs.

Script Note

The script excerpt is taken from a November 21, 2000 draft. In this draft the montage appears in Act Two, much later in the film.

Other Films

Apocalyse Now (opening thematic montage)

Falling Down (opening thematic montage)

Adaptation (2002) (Page 41, Scene 62)

Screenplay: Charlie Kaufman and Donald Kaufman, Draft: November 21, 2000.

Adapted from the book, *The Orchard Thief* by Susan Orlean.

MONTAGE

This sequence shows the entire history of mankind from a world sparsely populated with primitive hunter gathers to today's overcrowded technological society. We see the history of architecture, war, religion, commerce. We see murder and procreation. We see man interacting with his environment: farming, eating meat, admiring a view. We see old age and birth. We see it again and again at dizzying speed. We see Laroche as a child alone with his turtles. We see Orlean as a child alone with her diary. We see Alice serving food, smiling at customers. We finish on sad Kaufman getting into his car and leaving the Santa Barbara Orchid Show. The entire sequence takes two minutes.

1.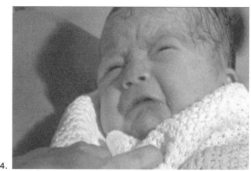

2.

3.

4.

5.

19. Film Element: Assembly

Assembly editing is a term that Alfred Hitchcock used in referring to the kind of editing used in *Psycho's* shower scene. In this case assembly means the creative construction of a scene through the assembly of separate pieces of film. The resulting scene being a kind of mosiac of shots producing a larger idea.

Film Example: *Psycho*

Cutting, as Hitchcock said in his 1959 televised interview for the Canadian Broadcasting Corporation, is a kind of severance (Hitchcock). It is also a kind of assembly.

In *Psycho*, Hitchcock intentionally differentiates the film's two murders by editing choices.

Shower Scene
In the shower scene, Hitchcock's purpose is to first shock us with the event of a murder and then horrify us with its brutality. In a rapid succession of cuts, 78 in 45 seconds, Hitchcock takes us past the shower curtain into the stall giving us the POV of the murderer. It's almost as though Hitchcock's exaggerated use of cutting intentionally refers back to the cutting of the victim.

Stairwell Scene
The second murder is shot and edited entirely differently. The focus is not on the brutality of the murderer, as we have already seen that. The focus is on whether or not the victim will be killed. Consequently, it's a suspense scene with our attention directed on the minutes preceding the murder, not the murder. In the second murder, the shots are long takes. Once the audience and the victim realize that the victim is about to be killed, the scene is over. Despite the fact that the methods of both murders were identical, the editing generates two entirely different emotional responses.

Dramatic Value

Editing can guide the emotional response of the viewer by choosing how to parcel out the event in shots over time.

Script Note

The script excerpt from the "shower scene" is included to show how highly stylized editing can be suggested without disrupting the mounting suspense.

Other Films

*Metropolis (*dream sequence)

Psycho (1960) (Shower Scene)

Screenplay: Joseph Stephano. Revised Draft, Dec. 1, 1959.
Novel: Robert Bloch.

INT. MARY IN SHOWER

Over the bar on which hangs the shower curtain, we can see the bathroom door, not entirely closed. For a moment we watch Mary as she washes and soaps herself.

There is still a small worry in her eyes, but generally she looks somewhat relieved.

Now we see the bathroom door being pushed slowly open.

The noise of the shower drowns out any sound. The door is then slowly and carefully closed.

And we see the shadow of a woman fall across the shower curtain. Mary's back is turned to the curtain. The white brightness of the bathroom is almost blinding.

Suddenly we see the hand reach up, grasp the shower curtain, rip it aside.

CUT TO:

MARY - ECU

As she turns in response to the feel and SOUND of the shower curtain being torn aside. A look of pure horror erupts in her face. A low terrible groan begins to rise up out of her throat. A hand comes into the shot. The hand holds an enormous bread knife. The flint of the blade shatters the screen to an almost total, silver blankness.

THE SLASHING

An impression of a knife slashing, as if tearing at the very screen, ripping the film. Over it the brief gulps of screaming. And then silence. And then the dreadful thump as Mary's body falls in the tub.

REVERSE ANGLE

The blank whiteness, the blur of the shower water, the hand pulling the shower curtain back. We catch one flicker of a glimpse of the murderer. A woman, her face contorted with madness, her head wild with hair, as if she were wearing a fright-wig. And then we see only the curtain, closed across the tub, and hear the rush of the shower water. Above the shower-bar we see the bathroom door open again and after a moment we HEAR the SOUND of the front door slamming.

CUT TO:

THE DEAD BODY

Lying half in, half out of the tub, the head tumbled over,touching the floor, the hair wet, one eye wide open as if popped, one arm lying limp and wet along the tile floor. Coming down the side of the tub, running thick and dark along the porcelain, we see many small threads of blood. CAMERA FOLLOWS away from the body, travels slowly across the bathroom, past the toilet, out into the bedroom. As CAMERA approaches the bed, we see the folded newspaper as Mary placed it on the bedside table.

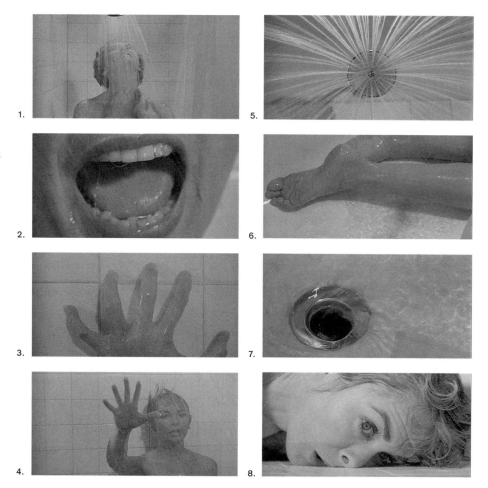

1.
2.
3.
4.
5.
6.
7.
8.

20. Film Element: *Mise-en-Scène*

Mise-en-scène is a French term meaning "putting in the scene," originally used to describe the physical production of the film. Today, however, mise-en-scène refers to a scene in which the action plays out in front of a continually running camera. New compositions are created through blocking, lens zooms and camera movement instead of cutting. The scene is shot in real time as one uninterrupted take that will stand on its own without the aid of editing.

Film Example: *Psycho* (Shower Scene Aftermath)

Right after *Psycho*'s shower scene, the cutting changes to mise-en-scène. Now we see Norman rushing from his mother's house to the cabin where Marion was killed. Once inside, the camera moves with Norman as he paces back and forth thinking about what to do with the body. When Norman enters another cabin to retrieve janitorial supplies, the camera continues to roll outside the door, until he returns with a mop and a bucket. When Norman re-enters the cabin we watch in real time as Norman drags the body onto the plastic sheeting. This is followed by Norman mopping out the tub and finally driving off with the body. Hitchcock's switch to mise-en-scène achieves a number of things.

Dramatic Value

Where the rapid assembly editing of the shower scene appeared constructed to add chaos and disorient, the mise-en-scène shots in the aftermath scene appear to return us to normalcy. The shots are long, smooth takes that spool out slowly in real time. However, the content sabotages any sense of relief. Seeing Norman carefully smooth out the plastic sheeting readying it for Marion's body, then sloshing her blood around the tub with a janitor's mop only serves to sustain our revulsion. We are supposed to feel soothed by the return to normalcy, but instead it heightens our fears.

Script Note

Take a look at how effortlessly the script exploits editing technique but does not call attention to technical details.

Other Films Using Mise-en-Scène Shots

Rope (entire film)

Touch of Evil (opening)

The Player (opening)

The 400 Blows (many shots throughout)

Historical Note

Hitchcock filmed *Rope* (1948) as one continuous *mise-en-scène* shot. The only breaks in filming occurred when he stopped for necessary magazine changes.

Psycho (1960) (Shower Scene Aftermath)

Screenplay: Joseph Stephano. Revised Draft, Dec. 1, 1959.

Novel: Robert Bloch.

EXT. THE PATH - (NIGHT)

Norman is coming AT CAMERA, running head-on. He dashes into an extreme close up and we see the terror and fear ripe in his face. CAMERA PANS as Norman races past, holds as Norman runs to the porch and quickly along it and directly to Mary's room.

INT. MARY'S CABIN - (NIGHT)

Norman pauses a moment in the doorway, glances about the room, hears the shower going, sees the bathroom door is open. He goes to the bathroom, looks in, sees the body.

Slowly, almost carefully, he raises his hands to his face, covers his eyes, turns his face away. Then he crosses to the window, looks out at the house. Shot is so angled that we see the bedside table with the newspaper on it.

After a moment, Norman moves from the window, sinks onto the edge of the bed.

FRESH ANGLE - BEHIND NORMAN

Norman sitting on bed, the bathroom in b.g. of shot. We can see only the hand of the dead girl, lying along the tile floor.

21. Film Element: Intercutting

Intercutting (also called cross-cutting) occurs when two scenes are shot in sequence, but presented by cutting back and forth between them. This creates a sense of two actions occurring simultaneously in two different locations. Frequently intercutting is used leading up to the climax scene in Act Three. Intercutting can also be used for other purposes. In *Cabaret*, winner of eight Academy Awards, intercutting is used at the end of Act Two to suggest change: in this case that of political climate. This is a tough abstract concept to convey without dialog. Here's how it was done in *Cabaret*.

Film Example: *Cabaret*

Set in Berlin during Hitler's rise, we first see the freewheeling world of the Berlin cabaret. As the film progresses, the Nazi's presence strengthens until finally, it has taken over the culture. The change of political climate is suggested in a dance number that adds intercutting to the end of the scene to make the inferences less abstract and more particular.

Part 1

The dance number starts like ones earlier in the movie. A kick-line of dancers perform, while the MC throws out sexual innuendoes to his audience. Then the change begins.

Part 2

The dancers stop. Each tears off the flowers pinned to their hats. They spin their hats around. The hats change from flirtatious to militaristic. Their dance steps change from chorus line kicks to the goose-stepping march of the Nazis. The orange yellow saturated lighting associated with the era's expressionism and freedom drains away. It's replaced by a chilling blue fog. Then the film begins to intercut.

Part 3

It cuts from the goose-stepping dancers to the home of a young Jewish woman. Each cut back to the woman's house steps up the brutality of the lawless thugs that have trespassed onto her property. First we see the thugs rush onto her gated property. Next, the woman stands bewildered at her doorway responding to late night callers who have disappeared. Lastly, we see her family dog lying dead on her doorstep. The brutal murder of her dog, grounds the abstract dance with a specific incident.

Dramatic Value

The intercutting goes from the abstract to the specific. It immediately sets up the idea that the old world is gone, and a new one has arrived. The violence of the Nazi thugs has become the norm and will go without punishment.

Script Note

The two scenes excerpted here were combined into one scene in the final film.

Other Films

Pulp Fiction, The Graduate, Thelma and Louise

Cabaret (1972)

Screenplay: Jay Presson Allen, First Draft June 7, 1970
Book: Christopher Isherwood, *Berlin Short Stories.*
Play: John van Druten, *I am a Camera.*

INT. KIT KLUB - NIGHT (Page 21-2)

CRASHINGLY LOUD BAVARIAN MUSIC - SHOW LIGHTS FULL UP

-KLUB AUDIENCE WILDLY ENTHUSIASTIC.

The MC, still in cabaret make-up, but now wearing shirt
and leiderhosen, is performing a traditional Bavarian
Slapdance... upon an unidentifiable GIRL PARTNER; he
smilingly administers face and body slaps in time to the
music. The comic violence of this dance should play in
juxtaposition to the inter-cut scenes of realistic violence.
Music cuts off on each quick cut to the mugging.

QUICK CUT TO:

MAX, being knocked to the ground, bloody, but silent still,
as the Nazis begin to kick him brutally.

QUICK CUT TO:

Shot of MC's feet in sturdy Bavarian boots as his feet
continue the rhythm of the slapdance.

QUICK CUT TO:

Shot of NAZI's feet, kicking MAX.

QUICK CUT TO:

Smiling MC, dancing, slapping, stomping.

QUICK CUT TO:

On the music's last beat, the YOUNG NAZI aims one

final kick at MAX, who rolls over in silent anguish.

INT. KIT KAT CLUB - NIGHT (Page 105)

The Kit Kat CHORUS GIRLS (about seven) enter the wings doing a typical "Tiller Girls" routine. Facing front, arms around each others' waists, unison kicking, etc. They are dressed in abbreviated costumes, revealing much flesh above their stocking tops and at the cleavage. Suddenly we are aware that one of the girls is the M.C.

(Note: This will be a version of the very effective number from the show in which the M.C. reveals himself to be a transvestite.)

As the dance begins to fall apart, we hear the ominous sounds of military drums. The music changes to a martial version of "TOMORROW BELONGS TO ME" as the M.C. and the GIRLS goose-step offstage.

1.

2.

3.

4.

5.

6.

22. Film Element: Split Screen

A split screen runs two shots side-by-side within a single frame. Like intercutting, a split screen creates the idea of simultaneous action. Split screen was a staple of the 1950s and 1960s. It was often used to depict phone conversations as in *Pillow Talk* that starred Rock Hudson and Doris Day. It was also used in classic horror films. Its use, however is not limited to genre. Recently Quentin Tarantino revived the split screen in his comic book–inspired film *Kill Bill Vol. 1*.

Film Example: *Kill Bill Vol. 1*

Black Mamba (Uma Thurman) lies comatose in a hospital bed. In having unexpectedly survived a brutal attempt on her life, an assassin is sent in to finish the job.

As the assassin, dressed as a nurse, walks toward Thurman's hospital bed, the film switches to split screen. By using split screen we are able to see both Thurman lying unconscious in bed and the approaching assassin at the same time.

Dramatic Value

Split screen can show two or more images on the screen at one time. It is most often used to suggest simultaneity, but is not limited to this. In this instance the split screen also suggests the imminent physical proximity of the victim to the assassin by having the two share the frame and appearing to almost touch. This serves to further heighten the suspense.

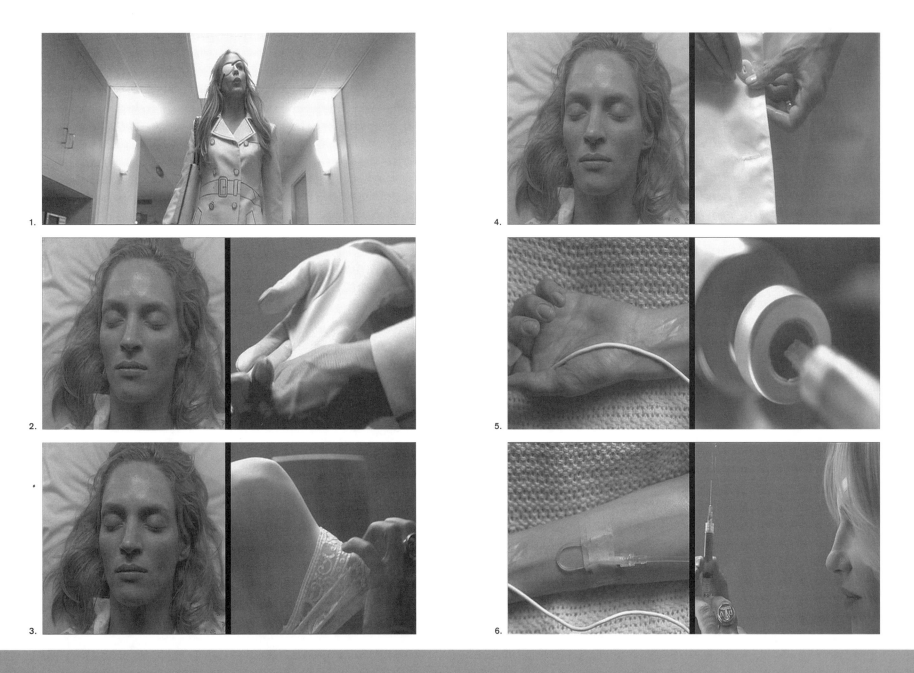

23. Film Element: Dissolves

Dissolves blend one shot into another. This is achieved optically by fading out the first shot while the second shot fades up. A dissolve softens a cut. Dissolves can be brief or extended depending how "soft" the filmmaker wants the effect to be. Dissolves have been a staple technique since the 1920s.

Film Example: *Citizen Kane*

In the script of *Citizen Kane*, Orson Welles and co-writer Herman Mankiewitz use dissolves to convey the idea of enormity. In the opening scene, the camera introduces Kane's estate, dissolving twelve times. Each dissolve shows us a different part of the estate. This underscores its magnitude. The implication is that no one shot could have encompassed the massive grounds, so multiple shots had to be taken.

Dramatic Value

A dissolves links two ideas together by blending one image into another. In this case multiple views of the estate are presented but remain connected by the use of dissolves. Dissolves offer endless dramatic possibilities. They are often used to show the passage of time.

Script Note

Although twelve dissolves were included in the script, due to space, only two of the twelve are included here.

Other Films

Metropolis (transformation of the heroine into an evil robot)

Barton Fink (arriving at the Hotel Earle, waves)

Citizen Kane (1941) (Page 1)

Screenplay: Herman J. Mankiewicz and Orson Welles.

```
EXT. XANADU - FAINT DAWN - 1940 (MINIATURE)
```

Window, very small in the distance, illuminated.

All around this is an almost totally black screen. Now, as the camera moves slowly towards the window which is almost a postage stamp in the frame, other forms appear; barbed wire, cyclone fencing, and now, looming up against an early morning sky, enormous iron grille work.

Camera travels up what is now shown to be a gateway of gigantic proportions and holds on the top of it - a huge initial "K" showing darker and darker against the dawn sky. Through this and beyond we see the fairy-tale mountaintop of Xanadu, the great castle a silhouette at its summit, the little window a distant accent in the darkness.

```
DISSOLVE:

(A SERIES OF SET-UPS, EACH CLOSER TO THE GREAT WINDOW, ALL TELLING
SOMETHING OF:)
```

The literally incredible domain of CHARLES FOSTER KANE.

Its right flank resting for nearly forty miles on the Gulf Coast, it truly extends in all directions farther than the eye can see. Designed by nature to be almost completely bare and flat - it was, as will develop, practically all marshland when Kane acquired and changed its face - it is now pleasantly uneven, with its fair share of rolling hills and one very good-sized mountain, all man-made. Almost all the land is improved, either through cultivation for farming purposes or through careful landscaping, in the shape of parks and lakes. The castle dominates itself, an enormous pile, compounded of several genuine castles, of European origin, of varying architecture - dominates the scene, from the very peak of the mountain.

```
DISSOLVE:

GOLF LINKS (MINIATURE)
```

Past which we move. The greens are straggly and overgrown, the fairways wild with tropical weeds, the links unused and not seriously tended for a long time.

```
DISSOLVE OUT:
```

1.

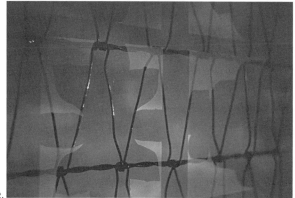

2.

3.

24. Film Element: Dissolves

As we discussed in the previous example, dissolves are created optically by blending two shots together by fading out the first, as the second shot fades up.

Film Example: *Barton Fink*

Barton Fink opens with the success of Barton's Broadway play. In the afterglow of his success we see Barton in a heated exchange with his agent who urges Barton to go to California and "cash in" on his fame. Barton adamantly refuses not wanting to leave New York or the common man , which are the wellsprings of his creativity.

First Shot

The dissolve reveals the outcome of their argument: an iconic image of waves crashing in the sunlit Pacific Ocean. Clearly the agent has won. Then we see an extended dissolve blending the ocean imagery with an unexpected location: the creepy foyer of the Hotel Earle.

Second Shot

The second image is anything but Hollywood. As the slow dissolve plays out, the floor of the hotel seems washed with the ocean. Then the ocean imagery dissolves away and Barton is left alone. It's as though Barton has been ejected from the ocean into the worn foyer — a fish-out-of-water. The dissolve works to contrast the iconic image of California against the new reality in which Barton has found himself. It also serves to underscore Barton's status as an outsider.

Dramatic Value

Endless dramatic possibilities. Often used in montages to indicate the passage of time. Dissolves also soften the cuts between images.

Other Films

Titanic (see Film Element 50)

Apocalypse Now (introduction of protagonist)

Adaptation (opening montage)

25. Film Element: Smash Cut

The purpose of a *smash cut* is to jar the audience with a sudden and unexpected change in image or sound. Here are two film examples of how a smash cut was created — there are many more methods used and many more yet to be invented.

Film Example: *American Beauty*

In *American Beauty*, the writer, Alan Ball, employs both visual and audio smash cuts to introduce protagonist Lester Burnham fast asleep in his suburban cocoon. Although the visuals suggested by the writer were greatly pared down by director Sam Mendes, the overall story elements were left in place.

The smash cut is created visually by going from an aerial wide shot to a close up of a clock. It was augmented aurally by going from silence to the blast of an alarm clock.

Film Example: *Psycho*

A smash cut can also be produced by cutting a wide shot against a huge close-up. The effect is like a loud visual bang. It jolts the audience by sabotaging their visual expectations. This was done in the stairway scene in *Psycho*. In this case it was also a high-angle.

Note: Another method is to splice a fast moving shot against a static shot. The audience feels like they are on a speeding train that just hit a cement wall.

Script Note

Writers will sometimes specifically spell out their intentions by using "smash cut to" between the two images or scenes. However, oftentimes, the writer will just juxtapose the two images without cueing the reader.

Dramatic Value

Like many other techniques, a smash cut underscores a scene. However, its purpose is to create a jarring, uncomfortable sensation for the audience. Used sparingly, it can be effective. If, however, the audience learns to expect it, it will feel hackneyed.

American Beauty (1999) (Page 8)

Screenplay: Alan Ball, 4/1/98.

```
EXT. SUBURB - EARLY MORNING

----

The boy on the bike watches in admiration. the MAN
slowly floats by above him and tousles his hair. The
dog BARKS. The man continues flying, rolling on his back
like a playful porpoise. The dog keeps BARKING... and we
SMASH CUT TO:

INT. BURNHAM HOUSE - MASTER BEDROOM - DAY

We HEAR the harsh BUZZ OF an ALARM CLOCK. Vic Damone
still sings "I'M NOBODY'S BABY" elsewhere in the house.
Outside, a dog is still BARKING.
```

1.

2.

American Beauty

Psycho (1960)

Screenplay: Joseph Stephano. Revised Draft, Dec. 1, 1959.

Novel: Robert Bloch.

```
INT. STAIRWAY AND UPSTAIRS LANDING

We see Arbogast coming up the stairs. And now we see,
too, the door of the mother's room, opening, carefully
and slowly.

As Arbogast reaches the landing, the door opens and the
mother steps out, her hand raises high, the blade of an
enormous knife flashing.

C.U. - A BIG HEAD OF AN ASTONISHED ARBOGAST

The knife slashes across his cheek and neck....
```

1.

2.

Psycho

Chapter Credits By Film Element

17. Citizen Kane (1941)
Writer: Herman J. Mankiewicz (Screenplay) and
Writer: Orson Welles (Screenplay)
Writer: John Houseman (Screenplay)
                           (Uncredited)
Director: Orson Welles
Production Company: Mercury Productions
Production Company: RKO Pictures
Distributor: RKO Pictures Inc. (1941) USA
                           Theatrical
Distributor: Warner Home Video (DVD)

18. Adaptation (2002)
Writer: Charlie Kaufman (Screenplay) and
Writer: Donald Kaufman (Screenplay)
Writer: Susan Orlean (Book: *The Orchid Thief*)

Director: Spike Jonz
Production Company: Beverly Detroit
Production Company: Clinica Estetico Ltd.
Production Company: Good Machine
Production Company: Magnet Productions
Production Company: Propaganda Films
Distributor: Columbia Pictures USA (Theatrical)
Distributor: Columbia/TriStar Home Video
                           2003 (DVD)

19. Psycho (1960)
Writer: Joseph Stephano
Writer: Robert Bloch (Novel)
Director: Alfred Hitchcock Production
Company: Shamley Productions
Distributor: Paramount Pictures
Distributor: Universal Home Entertainment
                           (USA) (DVD)

20. Psycho (1960)
Same as above.

21. Cabaret (1972)
Writer: Jay Presson Allen
Writer: Christopher Isherwood
                           (Book: *Berlin Short Stories*)
Writer: John van Druten (Play: *I am
                           a Camera*)
Writer: Joe Masteroff (Musical:
                           Cabaret)
Director: Bob Fosse
Production Company: ABC Circle Films
Production Company: American Broadcasting
                           Company (ABC)
Distributor: Allied Artists Pictures
                           Corporation
Distributor: Warner Home Video (USA)
                           (DVD)

22. Kill Bill: Vol. 1 (2003)
Writer: Quentin Tarantino (Screenplay)
Writer: QI and U1 (Character of the Bride)
Director: Quentin Tarantino
Production Company: Miramax Films
Production Company: A Band Apart
Production Company: Super Cool ManChu
Distributor: Miramax Films

23. Citizen Kane (1941)
Writer: Herman J. Mankiewicz
                           (Screenplay) and
Writer: Orson Welles (Screenplay)
Writer: John Houseman (Screenplay)
                           (Uncredited)
Director: Orson Welles

Production Company: Mercury Productions
Production Company: RKO Pictures
Distributor: RKO Pictures Inc. (1941)
                           USA Theatrical
Distributor: Warner Home Video
                           (DVD)

24. Barton Fink (1991)
Writer: Joel Coen (Screenplay) &
Writer: Ethan Coen (Screenplay)
Director: Joel Coen
Director: Ethan Coen (Uncredited)
Production Company: Circle Films Inc.
Production Company: Working Title Films
Distributor: 20th Century Fox Film
                           Corporation

25. American Beauty (1999)
Writer: Alan Ball
Director: Sam Mendes
Production Company: Dreamworks SKG
Production Company: Jinks/Cohen Company
Distributor: Dreamworks

SECTION **5**

TIME

TIME

A film is a *dramatic* representation of life. It is made up of scenes ordered to represent the passage of film time through the assembly of edited shots. Film time is rarely paced as we would experience it. With the exception of mise-en-scène, most edited sequences manipulate real time. As soon as we cut from one shot to another we have the opportunity of altering the experience of real time. We can speed it up, slow it down, freeze it, or disrupt it. We can also move backwards or forward.

The reason filmmakers alter time is because they are creating a dramatic story. Only those moments that contribute to its advancement are included, all else is left out.

Time Alteration within a Scene

Audiences have come to expect time alteration within a scene: A woman opens the door to a high rise. We see her briefly inside the ascending elevator. We then cut to her walking into a law office on the 35th floor. This is a staple editing technique to speed up time. Editing can also slow down an event by cutting to multiple reaction or insert shots. Both have become standard techniques that lend a lot of elasticity to a scene in terms of time manipulation.

Flashbacks and Flashforwards

Where there is less flexibility is when time periods change from scene to scene. While a single flashback or flashforward is rarely a problem, the continual interweaving of different time periods throughout a movie is a lot more difficult.

Limitations

By use of its narrator, a novelist can relay a character's reflections on his/her past or dreams of the future all in a single paragraph. Subsequent flashbacks to remembered dialog or imagined future actions can occur continuously throughout the story. This falls within the reader's expectations.

Unless the filmmaker borrows the novelist's narrator or uses extended dialog, it is extremely difficult to do this in a film. Cutting back and forth in time is usually too visually disruptive. Even if the filmmaker opts for narration or dialog-heavy passages, most audiences will soon get restless.

Despite the difficulty, flashbacks and flashforwards can offer a powerful tool. The following is a list of films that have used these tools to great effect.

Recommended Movies

Citizen Kane	*Sunset Boulevard*
Titanic	*Back to the Future*
Sorry, Wrong Number	*Groundhog Day*
To Kill a Mockingbird	*Raising Arizona*
Midnight Cowboy	*Run, Lola, Run*
Out of Africa	*The People vs. Larry Flynt*
Dolores Claiborne	*Adaptation*
Cape Fear	*American Beauty*

Recommended Study

Compare any novel, upon which a movie has been based, to the screenplay. Compare for example, the first ten pages of *Dances with Wolves*, the novel, to *Dances with Wolves*, the screenplay. Take a look at how much interweaving of time occurs in the novel. The narrator carries the reader back and forth, recreating the protagonist's memories while at the same time commenting on future aspirations. Then look at the screenplay. The screenplay's narrator is completely absent during the first ten pages. There are almost no references to the past or the future. The difference in how these two formats use time to tell the same story is especially striking when you consider that Michael Blake authored both versions. Comparing a novel to its script version will quickly demonstrate how differently novelists and screenwriters approach the use of dramatic tools.

The following films demonstrate different methods of using time dramatically.

Film Elements

26. Pacing	*Barton Fink*
27. Contrast of Time	*Pulp Fiction*
28. Expanding Time	*Pulp Fiction*
29. Slo-motion	*Raging Bull*
30. Fast-motion	*Amélie*
31. Flashback	*Sunset Boulevard*
32. Flashforward	*The People vs. Larry Flynt*
33. Freeze Frame	*Butch Cassidy and the Sundance Kid, Thelma and Louise, The 400 Blows*
34. Visual Foreshadowing	*The Piano*

26. Film Element: Expanding Time through Pacing

As audiences we expect time to spool out as we experience it. Disrupting the audience's expectation provides a creative opportunity. Altering time can be done in a number of ways. In the following example, taken from *Barton Fink*, pacing is used to slow down time and externalize the protagonist's anxiety about his new environment.

Film Example: *Barton Fink*

The Hotel Earle is the strange new home for recently arrived New York playwright, Barton Fink. The Coen brothers use the hotel to externalize Barton's discomfort in his new L.A. environment.

In the script pages that follow Barton, who is already ill at ease after registering with Chet, now enters the hotel elevator. Once inside the elevator, it's as though Barton has entered a parallel universe. Every action the elevator man makes is noticeably delayed. It's as though the elevator man lives in a different time zone where minutes and hours are generated from a different clock.

Dramatic Value

This technique suggests that the world is disjointed and somehow off-kilter. It adds suspense without dialog, leaving the audience to fear what might lie ahead. It also suggests that the time alteration might not be real, just a projection of Barton's own anxiety. This helps to further represent Barton's inner turmoil. Changing pacing within a scene serves to separate a scene into distinct parts and/or characters into distinct worlds.

Barton Fink (1991) (Act 1, Page 12)

Screenplay: Joel Coen & Ethan Coen, Feb. 19, 1990.

```
Barton is walking to the elevator.

ELEVATOR

Barton enters and sets down his bags.

An aged man with white stubble, wearing a greasy maroon uniform, sits on
a stool facing the call panel. He does not acknowledge Barton's presence.

After a beat:

                    BARTON
          . . . Six, please.

The elevator man gets slowly to his feet. As he pushes the door closed:

                    ELEVATOR MAN
          Next stop: Six.
```

1.

2.

3.

27. Film Element: Contrast of Time (Pacing and Intercutting)

By intercutting two separate scenes, a number of dramatic effects can be created. For example, comparison is the product of intercutting in *Thelma and Louise*'s introductory scene where the career choices of Thelma and Louise are established. Later their character differences are further externalized when we cut back and forth as the two women pack.

Intercutting can also be used to quicken the pace and heighten suspense. Here's an example from *Pulp Fiction*'s prelude to its "adrenalin shot" scene.

Film Example: *Pulp Fiction*

Setup: Vince races to his drug dealer's house terrified that Mia, his boss's wife, is going to O.D. in the front seat of his car.

Conflict: Vince desperately needs his drug dealer's help. But Lance, the drug dealer, thwarts Vince at every turn.

Vince's Shots
Vince spins into the scene driving his car toward the camera.

From here on Vince is seen in a tight close-up. His head fills the frame. He looks screen left and never changes his position. He looks like an unstoppable missile.

We then cut to Lance's house, where Lance, the slightly stoned drug dealer, munches on breakfast cereal while laughing at an old slap-stick comedy on TV.

Lance's Shots
Lance's shots are wide and loose and initially *mise-en-scène*. Lance's lackadaisical manner, coupled with his slovenly living room, makes the scene feel unfocused. Lance moves slowly in his bathrobe toward the phone. The wide shots and slow moments peak the suspense. Lance's slightly stoned manner and his combative nature further heighten the suspense.

We then cut back and forth between the two locations.

Dramatic Value

Each time we cut to Lance's house Vince hopes for the right answer, but each time he is stalled by the visuals and Lance's reaction. This makes Vince more desperate, and Lance more combative. Lance's shots are long and the results and their outcome unproductive. Vince's shots are quick and tight, and visually commanding. The dramatic value of the intercutting is used here to step-up the suspense. Notice that the suspense is also augmented by other techniques like contrast in movement, length of shots, and camera angles.

Pulp Fiction (1994)

Screenplay: Quentin Tarantino, May 1993.

Stories by: Quentin Tarantino & Roger Roberts Avary

```
26.   INT. LANCE'S HOUSE - NIGHT
```

At this late hour, Lance has transformed from a bon vivant drug dealer to a bathrobe creature.

He sits in a big comfy chair, ratty blue gym pants, a worn-out but comfortable tee-shirt that has, written on it, "TAFT, CALIFORNIA," and a moth-ridden terry cloth robe. In his hand is a bowl of Cap'n Crunch with Crunch Berries. In front of him on the coffee table is a jug of milk, the box the Cap'n Crunch with Crunch Berries came out of, and a hash pipe in an ashtray.

On the big-screen TV in front of the table is the Three Stooges, and they're getting married.

> PREACHER (EMIL SIMKUS)
> (on TV)
> Hold hands, you love birds.

The phone RINGS.

Lance puts down his cereal and makes his way to the phone.

It RINGS again.

Jody, his wife, CALLS from the bedroom, obviously woken up.

> JODY (OS)
> Lance! The phone's ringing!

> LANCE
> (calling back)
> I can hear it!

> JODY (OS)
> I thought you told those fuckin' assholes never to call this late!

> LANCE
> (by the phone)
> I told 'em and that's what I'm gonna tell this fuckin' asshole right now!
>
> (he answers the phone)
> Hello, do you know how late it is? You're not supposed to be callin' me this fuckin' late.

BACK TO VINCENT IN THE MALIBU

Vincent is still driving like a stripe-assed ape, clutching the phone to his ear. WE CUT BACK AND FORTH during the conversation.

1.

4.

2.

5.

3.

6.

28. Film Element: Expanding Time — Overlapping Action

Movies have rhythms made up of a number of variables, one of which is film time. Expanding film time by overlapping action can add great dramatic value to a scene. It can shine a light on a particular moment or an entire scene. It is often used to underscore important plot twists, climactic scenes, and pivotal emotional revelations. Expanding film time is conventionally used to evoke suspense.

One way screenwriters and directors expand film time is by overlapping the action. For this to work they need to design the scene with enough cutaways and reaction shots to cut to. In this way, time can be stopped by extending the time it takes for the moment to play out on screen. This is done by showing the audience the same moment from different camera angles and points of view.

Film Example: *Pulp Fiction*

One of the most suspenseful scenes in *Pulp Fiction* is the "adrenalin shot" scene where Vincent stabs overdosed Mia, hoping to save her. If the scene had been depicted in real time, it would have taken about three seconds to play out. In fact the main character, Vincent, actually counts out the three seconds in the scene. Yet the filmed moment actually takes about forty seconds of screen time. This is thirteen times longer than the dialog suggests. Take a look at the scripted excerpt and see how Quentin Tarantino paces out this pivotal event through the use of multiple angles and reaction shots.

Dramatic Value

By expanding time, Tarantino tells the audience that the scene is important. Time is completely slowed down in such a way that it's as though each shot is a breath. The audience absorbs the rhythm of the editing; breathing with Vincent, his anxiety becomes ours, as we watch Vincent prepare to plunge the needle into Mia's chest.

Script Note

Notice in the scripted excerpt that each sentence is a shot. Without it being called out specifically, you can tell whether a shot is a close-up, medium shot, or wide-angle because of content.

Other Films

Psycho (shower scene)

Silence of the Lambs (climax scene)

Pulp Fiction (1994) (Page 62)

Screenplay: Quentin Tarantino, May 1993.

Stories by: Quentin Tarantino & Roger Roberts Avary

Vincent lifts the needle up above his head in a stabbing motion. He looks down on Mia.

Mia is fading fast. Soon nothing will help her.

Vincent's eyes narrow, ready to do this.

> VINCENT
> Count to three.

Lance, on this knees right beside Vincent, does not know what to expect.

> LANCE
> One...

RED DOT on Mia's body.

Needle raised ready to strike.

> LANCE (OS)
> ...two...

Jody's face is alive with anticipation.

NEEDLE in the air, poised like a rattler ready to strike.

> LANCE (OS)
> ...three!

The needle leaves frame, THRUSTING down hard.

Vincent brings the needle down hard, STABBING Mia in the chest.

Mia's head if JOLTED from the impact.

The syringe plunger is pushed down, PUMPING the adrenalin out through the needle.

Mia's eyes POP WIDE OPEN and she lets out a HELLISH cry of the banshee. She BOLTS UP in a sitting position, needle stuck in her chest -- SCREAMING.

1.

2.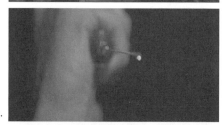

3.

4.

5.

6.

7.

8.

9.

10.

29. Film Element: Slo-Motion

Slo-motion is usually created in-camera by running the film through the gate faster than the standard 24 frames per second used to represent real time. This effect can create a number of heightened dramatic ideas.

One of the hallmark characteristics of slo-motion is that it can visually suggest two states of consciousness by contrasting it to real time. In this example from *Raging Bull*, it is used to separate normalcy and trauma.

Film Example: Raging Bull

In Martin Scorsese's *Raging Bull*, we go inside the ring with Jake La Motta to see the slo-motion brutality of the boxing world as Jake is pummeled to near death. The speed switches to slo-motion as Jake becomes weakened. The audience sees the world from behind Jake's eyeballs until the final blow is delivered.

Dramatic Value

Slowing down reality is often used to show how a character sees the world when in the midst of a traumatic event. This draws our attention to the scene. When slo-motion is coupled with a POV shot it can greatly increase audience sympathy.

1.

2.

3.

4.

30. Film Element: Fast-Motion (Time Compression)

Fast-motion compresses reality by having the film pass through the gate at a slower rate than the standard 24 frames per second. As it breaks the veneer of reality, fast-motion scenes are immediately separated from the rest of the film. Consequently, fast-motion is reserved for those moments that need to be especially highlighted. Fast-motion is often used in comedy, but can also be effective in drama. The examples below are taken from two films: the first is magical realism, the second, a dark comedy.

Film Example: *Amélie*

In Amélie, written by Guillaume Laurant and Jean-Pierre Jeunet, Amélie is a whimsical character who anonymously meddles in the lives of others to bring them unexpected joy. As the film is shot in the style of magical realism, director Jeunet frequently uses exaggerated effects like fast-motion. In these excerpted frames Amélie forges a letter from her landlady's lover to help the landlady heal a broken heart.

Film Example: *Requiem for a Dream* (not pictured)

In Darren Aronofsky's highly stylized film based on the novel by Hubert Selby, Jr., fast- motion is cleverly used to convey the shoddy treatment that protagonist Sara, receives from her doctor. The doctor approaches Sara in the outer offices in fast-motion. He simply ups her prescription and leaves. The effect of the speeded-up action underscores the doctor's inattention and the inevitability of Sara's descent.

Dramatic Value

Fast-motion both compresses time and separates the fast-motion scene from the rest of the film. For this reason it is used when emphasis is intended.

1.

2.

3.

4.

5.

31. Film Element: Flashback

A *flashback* is a staple technique in novels and plays. In movies it is used more sparingly as it risks taking us out of the forward-moving plot. The purpose of the flashback is to fill the audience in on important backstory. Many screenwriting books advise against them, arguing that flashbacks are an obvious catch-up device. It's true they are a "catch-up device"; in fact, that is precisely their function. Whether they are effective or not, however, depends entirely on their rendering.

Backstory is a very difficult problem for filmmakers. Without the luxury of the narrator there are limited ways to present the past. Flashbacks are one way to solve the problem.

The key to whether a flashback works is whether the flashback moves the plot forward. If it puts the film artificially on hold, is obviously dropped in the movie "just in time," or is aesthetically hackneyed, the audience will reject it. There are, however, too many beautifully rendered flashbacks to justify rejecting the device outright. The list below contains movies that use flashbacks. They represent some of the most acclaimed films in cinema history. Let's take a look at one such film, *Sunset Boulevard*, and see how it put the flashback to use.

Film Example: *Sunset Boulevard*

In the classic film *Sunset Boulevard*, we first meet the protagonist by way of his voice over. He tells us that a Hollywood screenwriter has just died and the police are investigating. In a few cuts we learn that the narrator is in fact the dead screenwriter. We then meet the narrator. He is the corpse floating upside-down in a Beverly Hills pool.

The rest of the movie is told as a flashback from the dead screenwriter. His objective is to tell us how he came to his end.

Dramatic Value

Backstory.

Other Films

Citizen Kane
Sorry, Wrong Number
To Kill a Mockingbird
Midnight Cowboy
Out of Africa
Dolores Claiborne
Cape Fear

Sunset Boulevard (1950)

Writers: Charles Brackett, Billy Wilder, D.M. Marshman, Jr. Script Version: March 21, 1949.

1.

2.

A-1
Thru
A-7

Start with sidewalk credits, music, camera moving
down the street as credits play out, then at finish,
pan up to street and see Coroner's hearse turning into
Norma's. Narration begins as credits finish and
Camera pans up, sirens screaming--

GILLIS' VOICE

Yes, this is Sunset Boulevard,
Los Angeles, California. It's
about five o'clock in the morning.

cops,
hearse,
bike cops,
all turning
into driveway…

That's the homicide squad. Complete
with detectives and newspapermen.
A murder has been reported from one
of those great, big houses in the
ten thousand block. You'll read
about it in the late editions. I'm
sure. You'll get it over your
radios, and see it on television.

EXT. NORMA'S
cops arriving,
drive up to
house, men
getting out,
camera pans
as they walk
around to
the pool…

Because an old time star is involved.
One of the biggest. But before
you hear it all distorted, and blown
out of proportions. Before those
Hollywood columnists get their hands
on it, maybe you'd like to hear the
facts, the whole truth. If so, you've
come to the right party. You see the
body of a young man was found floating
in the pool of her mansion. With
two shots in his back, and one in

UNDERWATER
SHOT OF GILLIS
face down in
pool, flashing
pictures taken
from above…

his stomach. Nobody important really,
just a movie writer, with a couple
of B-pictures to his credit. The
poor dope, he always wanted a pool.
Well, in the end he got himself a
pool, only the price turned out to
be a little high. Let's go back

DISSOLVE:
EXT. GILLLIS'
APT. IN
HOLLYWOOD

about six months and find the day
when it all started. I was living
in an apartment house above Franklin
and Ivar. Things were tough at the
moment. I hadn't worked in a studio
for a long time. So I sat there grinding
out original stories. Two a week.
Only I seemed to have lost my touch.
Maybe they weren't original. All I
know is, they didn't sell.

32. Film Element: Flashforward

A *flashforward* is a cut to the future. We can start in the past and flashforward to the present, or start in the present and flashforward to the future, real or imagined. A flashforward is typically assisted with a slow dissolve to prepare the audience for the time change.

In *The People vs. Larry Flynt,* writers Scott Alexander and Larry Karaszewski deliver an original take on the convention that's both organic to the scene and dramatically effective.

Film Example: *The People vs. Larry Flynt*

In the aftermath of being shot, Larry Flynt experiences chronic pain. Deadening the pain with drugs, Flynt soon finds himself addicted. Soon Flynt's wife joins him and the two are unable to lift themselves out of their "narcotic fog."

The flashforward scene begins with the clang of their bedroom door slamming shut. In this case the door is a huge, steel security door with a locking system. Once locked, everyone, including the audience, is kept out. The camera remains on the door as a text generator scrolls through the months and years that pass. When five years is up, the door reopens.

Dramatic Value

The flashforward not only tells us that time has passed, but also characterizes the passage of time for the audience. It's a brilliant economic and story-advancing use of the device.

Script Note

For a superb example of a script treatment, see the published version of *The People vs. Larry Flynt* (Newmarket Shooting Script Series, 1996.) The treatment, originally sent to Oliver Stone in the form of a letter, is brilliant in its economy and its ability to convey, in a brief three pages, how the movie will play on the screen. Writers Scott Alexander and Larry Karaszewki have given their readers an invaluable template with which to conquer the difficult task of treatment writing.

The People vs. Larry Flynt (1996)

Screenplay: Scott Alexander & Larry Karaszewski, Revised First Draft, 1994.

INT. BEDROOM

ANGLE - ALTHEA

No reply. She listens to the miserable wailing. Althea stares at Larry, then at the needle in her hand.

She thinks, then refills the syringe and rolls up her own sleeve. Althea injects herself. As the drug consumes her body, she starts shivering uncontrollably. Althea climbs into bed and lies down next to Larry…

A pause, then she reaches over and hits a BUTTON.

OUTSIDE THE BEDROOM

A hulking 500-pound STEEL DOOR swings shut and locks with a thud.

                                        FADE OUT:

FADE IN:

The vaultlike door is still closed.

A SUPER appears: "FIVE YEARS LATER. 1983

INT. BEDROOM

The room has become a chamber of horrors: Dirty, dark, and clammy. Years of insane drug use have aged Althea and Larry beyond belief: Larry looks wasted and put on a bloated 50 pounds. Althea is gaunt, haggard, and a punked-out junkie. She wears a nose ring, and track marks run up and down her arms.

They converse in an incoherent, narcotic fog.

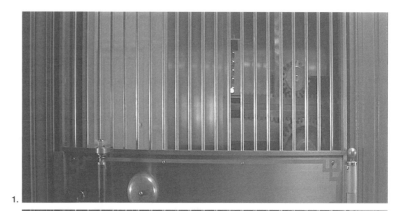

1.

2.

3.

33. Film Element: Freeze-Frame

A *freeze-frame* is created when a single frame appears "frozen" on the screen. This is achieved by repeatedly reprinting the frame, then letting it play out over time. In separating one image from the rest of the moving images, and having the audience view the frame like a photograph, the image takes on an iconic air. In *Kill Bill Vol. 1* Uma Thurman's character is given a freeze frame when she recalls being shot. By freezing the moment, the audience is cued to take special notice of the content.

In the three films reviewed below, freeze-frame is also used for emphasis. In these films, the freeze-frame is used at the end of the film, leaving us with a single emblematic impression of the protagonist.

Film Examples: *Butch Cassidy and the Sundance Kid, Thelma and Louise, The 400 Blows*

In *Butch Cassidy and the Sundance Kid* and *Thelma and Louise*, the audience comes to love the protagonists who are most probably about to die. Rather than see their beloved characters face the final moments of their life, the writers/directors freeze the characters, so they can live forever.

The same technique is used in *The 400 Blows*, where the young protagonist has just run away from reform school. Having used all available options, he heads for the beach. Rather than see him further brutalized by his circumstances, the film leaves us with his frozen image.

Dramatic Value

By halting the image, the freeze-frame suspends a character or action in time. Though we may suspect what will happen next, we won't ever know. The event will never unfold, and the characters will never grow, change — or die. In freezing the characters, it protects them from time. When placed at the end of the movie, it gives the audience a final visual picture, a kind of emblematic summary to take away with them.

Other Films

Blood Simple (final shot)

Kill Bill Vol. 1 (moment of realization)

Butch Cassidy and the Sundance Kid (1969)

Screenplay: William Goldman, 1969.

```
CLOSE-UP - THE CAPTAIN
```

Over and over as he gestures forward toward the tiny room where Butch and Sundance are:

```
                    CAPTAIN
          Ataque-Ataque-Ataque-
```

Cut to:

One group of men, vaulting the wall, moving forward and quickly.

Cut to:

Another group of men and another, all of them vaulting the wall and starting to run and-

Cut to:

```
CLOSE-UP - BUTCH and SUNDANCE
```

The Camera freezes them. And as it does, a tremendous fusilage of shots is heard, then another, even louder, and more and more shots, building its tempo and sound. The shots continue to sound.

Butch and Sundance remain frozen.

Final fade-out

THE END

Butch Cassidy and the Sundance Kid

Thelma and Louise

The 400 Blows

34. Film Element: Visual Foreshadowing

Visual foreshadowing is when a visual symbol, planted early, suggests an action that will take place later in the film. Here's how it was used in Jane Campion's *The Piano*.

Film Example: *The Piano*

At the end of Act Two, Ada, the female protagonist in Jane Campion's *The Piano*, is punished for betraying her husband. Her husband takes an ax and chops off one of Ada's fingers.

The brutal scene is foreshadowed earlier in the film in a shadow play. At the end of Act One, a local Reverand and Ada's sisters-in-law participate in rehearsing a shadow play. The play's action mimics the later plot point almost identically in shadows.

Though the first scene sets up the foreshadowing, the audience is only cognizant of it when the second scene provides the pay off.

Dramatic Value

Foreshadowing sets up expectations in the audience. In this case the play sets up both the physical action and the societal values that will be called up later in the film.

Other Films

Back to the Future (clocks in opening scene)

The Piano (1993)

Screenplay: Jane Campion, 4th Draft 1991.

Sc 59   INT   MISSION HOUSE   NIGHT

Inside the REVEREND is closely watched by STEWART, AUNT MORAG and
NESSIE as he cuts out the shape of an axe from a piece of marbled
cardboard. A lamplight flickers warm tones across their faces while
the rest of the room is dark giving it a conspiratorial air.

> REVEREND
> Nessie, your hand out ... out
> here, please.

> NESSIE
> Oh, no use Mr. Stewart, I can't
> act.

> REVEREND
> Nessie, please.

NESSIE hesitatingly puts her arm out towards him and the REVEREND
chops away in the air two feet in front other, NESSIE looks at AUNT
MORAG puzzled.

> REVEREND
> Look you are being attacked!

The REVEREND points to the opposite rose-papered wall, where his
shadow and paper axe now look very real as they loom large above the
crouching NESSIE chopping into her. NESSIE squeals, as does MARY.

> REVEREND
> And with the blood ... it will
> be a good effect:

Sc 60   INT   BAINES' HUT   DAY

ADA's finger plays the fourth black key from the left hand side,
denoting lesson four.

1.

2.

3.

Chapter Credits By Film Element

26. *Barton Fink* (1991)

Writer:	Joel Coen (Screenplay) &
Writer:	Ethan Coen (Screenplay)
Director:	Joel Coen
Director:	Ethan Coen (Uncredited)
Production Company:	Circle Films Inc.
Production Company:	Working Title Films
Distributor:	20th Century Fox Film Corporation

27. *Pulp Fiction* (1994)

Writer:	Quentin Tarantino (Screenplay)
Writer:	Quentin Tarantino (Stories) &
Writer:	Robert Avary (Stories)
Director:	Quentin Tarantino
Production Company:	A Band Apart
Production Company:	Jersey Films
Production Company:	Miramax Films
Distributor:	Miramax Home Entertainment (USA) (DVD)

28. *Pulp Fiction* (1994)
Same as above.

29. *Raging Bull* (1980)

Writer:	Paul Shrader (Screenplay) &
Writer:	Mardik Martin (Screenplay)
Writer:	Jake La Motta (Book) &
Writer:	Joseph Carter (Book) &
Writer:	Peter Savage (Book)
Director:	Martin Scorsese
Production Company:	Chartoff-Winkler Productions
Distributor:	United Artists
Distributor:	MGM Home Entertainment (USA) (DVD)

30. *Amélie* (2001)

Writer:	Guillame Laurant, Jean-Pierre Jeunet (Screenplay)
Writers:	Guillame Laurant, Jean-Pierre Jeunet (Story)
Director:	Jean-Pierre Jeunet
Production Company:	Filmstiftung Nordhein-Westfalen
Production Company:	France 3 Cinema
Production Company:	La Sofica Sofinergie 5
Production Company:	Le Studio Canal+
Production Company:	MMC Independent GmblH
Production Company:	Tapioca Films
Production Company:	UGC Images
Production Company:	Victories Productions
Distributor:	Miramax

31. *Sunset Boulevard* (1950)

Writer:	Charles Brackett (Screenplay) &
Writer:	Billy Wilder (Screenplay) &
Writer:	D.M Marshman, Jr. (Screenplay)
Director:	Billy Wilder
Production Company:	Paramount Pictures
Distributor:	Paramount Pictures

32. *The People vs. Larry Flynt* (1996)

Writer:	Scott Alexander (Screenplay) &
Writer:	Larry Karaszewski (Screenplay)
Director:	Milos Forman
Production Company:	Columbia Pictures
Production Company:	Filmhaus
Production Company:	Illusion Entertainment
Production Company:	Ixtlan Corporation
Production Company:	Phoenix Pictures
Distributor:	Columbia TriStar

33. *Butch Cassidy and the Sundance Kid* (1969)

Writer:	William Goldman
Director:	George Roy Hill
Production Company:	20th Century Fox
Production Company:	Campanile
Distributor:	CBS/Fox
Distributor:	20th Century Fox Home Entertainment

34. *The Piano* (1993)

Writer:	Jane Campion
Director:	Jane Campion
Production Company	Australian Film Commission, CiBy, New South Wales Film and Television Office
Distributor:	Miramax Films

SECTION **6**

SOUND
EFFECTS

SOUND EFFECTS

Introduction

Outside of the musical score, movies rely on three kinds of sound to tell their stories:

Dialog

Voiceover

Sound Effects

Sound Effects and the Writer

While voiceover and dialog are well understood to be writers' tools, few screenwriters approach sound effects with the same certainty. Yet sound effects are as much the purview of the writer as are visual symbols. In the same way a writer can create an extended visual metaphor, sound effects can also suggest an extended aural metaphor. They can add layers of meaning to a film that are hard to achieve in other ways.

Sound effects can be obvious or quite subtle. They can intentionally draw attention to themselves, or manipulate with stealth. They can expose, disguise, suggest, establish, or reveal. They can also be tagged to specific events or characters.

Kinds of Sound Effects

Sound that is organic to a scene is often called *diegetic* sound. These sound effects can be realistic or altered for effect. External sound effects, those not logically heard in the scene, can also be added for dramatic value. These external sound effects, that is, those not part of the story world, are called *non-diegetic*.

For our purposes we can divide sound effects into four categories as follows.

Realistic
This is any sound effect that one could naturally expect to hear if situated in the filmed scene. The source of the sound might be on screen or off screen. Adding the most common sound effects like a car honking, a metronome, or a buzzing mosquito can greatly change the feeling of a scene.

Expressive
For our purposes an expressive sound effect is one that is realistic, but has been altered. This might mean that a phone's ring starts out normally and suddenly gets louder and louder. The sound comes from the scene but has been manipulated for effect.

Surreal
Sound effects are often enlisted to externalize a character's inner thoughts, nightmares, hallucinations, dreams, or wishes. We might hear, for example, the laughter of a child as a woman picks up a doll from childhood. This gives the scene a surreal feeling. This effect is often called *meta-diegetic*.

External
This is a sound effect that clearly does not come from the scene. It is an effect that is not heard or responded to by the characters. For example, if a character is making his last walk down death row, and slowly the audience hears a church bell, and we know there is no church for miles, we consider this sound external to the story world. The purpose of the sound effect is to signal the audience to the meaning of the scene. This kind of effect is known as *non-diegetic*.

Although the sound editors contribute the bulk of these effects in most movies, a writer can suggest an aural metaphor or the tone of the audio world. These effects should be used sparingly and should not dominate the writing. The director might add to these ideas or alter them as he or she would do with any other part of the script. However, when used purposefully they are as potent a storytelling tool as a movie's dialog or visuals.

Here are some ideas to consider when thinking about the use of sound effects:

— they can be used as an important "prop" or plot point

— sound and picture don't have to match

— realistic sound can be altered to behave expressively

— sound effects can be used to express internal thoughts of characters

— they can be used as a character's signature, or remind us of an event.

— they can be entirely external to the scene

— two sound effects, like a match cut in picture, can be placed side by side and generate an entirely new third idea (see Audio Transitions).

Here are the examples we will look at in this section:

Film Elements

35. Realistic Sound (Diegetic) (Character)		*Klute*
36. Realistic Sound (Diegetic) (Emotional Response)		*ET*
37. Expressive Sound (Diegetic) (Outer World)		*Barton Fink*
38. Surreal Sound (Meta-Diegetic) (Inner World)		*Barton Fink*

35. Film Element: Realistic Sound (Diegetic) (Character)

Realistic sound, also known as diegetic sound, is sound that would logically exist in the audio world depicted on the screen. In the critically acclaimed *Klute*, scripted by Andy and Dave Lewis, diegetic sound is cleverly used to reveal character.

Script Example: *Klute*

In Act Three, former call girl Bree Daniels (Jane Fonda) unknowingly finds herself face-to-face with a murderer. When a nearby phone suddenly rings, Fonda startles. But as Fonda looks over at the man beside her, she notices that he has registered no reaction. The man's lack of response cues her that he is in fact the murderer. Although this scene was altered in the movie, sound was again used to reveal character. This time the drama was racheted up by replacing the sound of the ringing phone with the taped recording of a woman dying.

Film Example: *Klute*

In the filmed version, Jane Fonda is seated across from the antagonist. The antagonist forces her to listen to an audiotape he has brought with him. As the tape progresses, Fonda realizes she is listening to her friend's murder. When Fonda looks over at the man, Fonda sees that he is completely unmoved by the woman's screams. At that moment Fonda realizes that the tape is serving as foreplay to murder — and that she is the next victim.

Dramatic Value

In both cases, the antagonist's lack of response to a sound is used to reveal character. Suspense is created as we watch the protagonist decode the antagonist's response. The turning point occurs when the protagonist succeeds, prompting a new action.

Other Films

Seven (metronome)

ET (sound of the trucks)

Klute (1971) (Scene 104, Page 114)

Screenplay: Andy Lewis, Dave Lewis, 1971.

The excerpt is taken mid-scene.

```
104.    INT. GARMENT BUILDING - NIGHT
----
                    CABLE
                  (continued)
          Her black book, Jane McKenna's, her
          list of -- of persons. I was told
          you're negotiating for it on her behalf --
```

The PHONE RINGS, an explosive noise. Bree startles. It
has been put on night-ring, to sound all over the loft,
and the noise is deafening. But -- the most bizarre
element is Cable's absolute lack of response to it. It
rings and rings as he talks and talks -- in the same
expository tone as before, without raising his voice.
It drowns out most of his words -- <u>at most we catch</u>
<u>only odd phrases of all the following</u> -- but he seems
not to hear it any more than the clamor of other things
torturing his soul.

1.

2.

3.

4.

5.

6.

36. Film Element: Realistic Sound (Diegetic) (Emotional Response)

Different sounds evoke different emotional responses. The sound of knocking on wood is generally positive, the sound of metal against metal, negative.

In the celebrated script of *ET*, Melissa Mathison exploits our built-in bias against metallic sounds in creating the "key men," ET's first antagonists.

Film Example: *ET*

In the opening scenes of Act One, a gang of humans arrive in huge ominous trucks intent on capturing ET. When the humans emerge they are faceless, shot from the waist down. They carry huge keys on their waistbands that jangle as they rush out in pursuit of ET. The sound of the keys is immediately coded as the sound of the approaching antagonists. Notice how Mathison specifically names one of the antagonists "Keys" in the script excerpt that follows.

Dramatic Value

By giving the antagonists a sound tag, the audience can judge how close they are to their victim, whether they are closing in or losing ground, regardless if they appear on screen or not. This forces the audience to participate, mimicking the action of the victim, in carefully listening to sound cues so they can quantify what distance lies between the antagonist and the hero. In this way sound can encourage a heightened level of audience participation as well as raising suspense.

Other Films

One Flew Over the Cuckoo's Nest (keys)

Seven (metronome)

ET (sound of the trucks)

ET (1982) (Pages 5-6)

Screenplay: Melissa Mathison, Rev. Sept. 8, 1981, Shooting Script.

24. THE CREATURE'S POV: THE CAR DOOR

The car door opens and a man steps out. Seen only from the waist down are: dark pants, heavy boots and a huge ring of KEYS hanging from his belt.

The KEYS make a tremendous racket, displacing all other sounds of the night.

25. REVERSE: THE CREATURE

THE CREATURE slides under cover just as his RED LIGHT COMES ON. We see a glimmer of it through shrubbery. His hand moves in to cover it.

26. WIDER: MORE CARS

More cars converge on the scene. We SEE bright HEADLIGHTS and HEAR slamming doors, muffled voices. Then we HEAR THE CREATURE break a branch from a shrub. He holds it against his chest. THE SOUND OF KEYS.

The sudden shafts of flashlight beams encircle the road and shoot out into the trees.

THE CREATURE moves unnoticed along the hillside. He crosses the road.

27. EXT. RAVINE - NIGHT - LONG SHOT

We see shadows of men jumping the ravine and heading into the forest. THE CREATURE hides in the near end of the shallow ravine.

KEYS is the last to jump.

The SOUND of KEYS is hideous.

1.

2.

3.

37. Film Element: Expressive Sound (Diegetic) (Outer World)

Expressive diegetic sound is sound that is organic to the scene but has been altered for dramatic effect. The example below is taken from the Coen brothers' *Barton Fink*.

Film Example: *Barton Fink*

As Barton waits to check in at a seedy hotel in L.A., he rings the bell on the unattended counter. At first the bell rings exactly as we would expect. But then the bell keeps ringing. Barton scans the lobby for some kind of explanation. Suddenly, Chet, the hotel's bell boy, pops up from a trap door behind the reception desk. The bell keeps ringing. Without acknowledging the strangeness of the ringing, Chet finally places a dirty finger on top of the bell, silencing it.

Here sound adds to the strangeness of the hotel and externalizes Barton's discomfort in his new location. The audience shares Barton's anxiety as they can't explain the bell either.

Film Example: *Barton Fink*

A few scenes later the Coen brothers use the same technique again. This time it's the hum of a mosquito. When Barton enters his room at the Hotel Earle, we hear humming. At first the sound is natural, but then it changes. The humming fades in and out as though the mosquito itself has an agenda. As the scene continues the mosquito seems to be intentionally taunting its guest.

Dramatic Value

By using two simple sounds expressively, those of a bell and a mosquito, the Coen brothers make us fear for the protagonist. By connecting the sound clues, along with other clues, the audience starts extrapolating. We wonder what "bad things" await.

Script Note

Script excerpts from both scenes are included on the accompanying page.

Other Films

ET
Apocalypse Now
Psycho
Single White Female

Barton Fink (1991)

Screenplay: Joel Coen & Ethan Coen, Feb. 19, 1990.

Ringing Bell Scene (Page 10)

```
Barton moves toward the front desk.

THE REVERSE

As Barton stops at the empty desk. He hits a small silver
bell next to the register. Its ring-out goes on and on without
losing volume.

After a long beat there is a dull scuffle of shoes on stairs.
Barton, puzzled, looks around the empty lobby, then down at the
floor behind the front desk.

A TRAP DOOR

It swings open and a young man in a faded maroon uniform,
holding a shoebrush and a shoe - not one of his own - climbs up
from the basement.

He closes the trap door, steps up to the desk and sticks his
finger out to touch the small silver bell, finally muting it.

The lobby is now silent again.
```

Mosquito Scene (Page 15)

```
BARTON'S POV

A naked, peeling ceiling.

The hum - a mosquito, perhaps - stops.

BARTON

His eyes move this way and that. After a silent beat, he shuts
them again.

After another silent beat, we hear - muffled, probably from an
adjacent room - a brief, dying laugh. It is sighing and weary,
like the end of a laughing fit, almost a sob.

Silence again.

We hear the rising mosquito hum.
```

1.

2.

3.

38. Film Element: Surreal Sound (Meta-Diegetic) (Inner World)

Meta-diegetic is any sound that represents a character's inner world, such as nightmares, dreams, hallucinations, wishes, and so on. In this scene from *Barton Fink*, it appears that Barton is transferring an inner wish onto the scene depicted in a postcard.

Film Example: *Barton Fink*

When Barton enters his room at the Hotel Earle, he enters guardedly. His anxiety has already been set off in registering downstairs with Chet. As Barton enters his room, his anxiety is further heightened. Everything in the room, like the lobby, seems to be off kilter. The bed squeaks louder than expected, the windows don't open, and the wall paper oozes a gooey syrup, appearing almost organic.

Then Barton notices a postcard tacked to the wall. It's an iconic image of a California girl sunbathing on the beach.

Barton focuses on the postcard. Now we hear gulls and waves crashing. It is as though we have been transplanted to the beach. From the context and sound effects, we assume that Barton is projecting some kind of inner wish onto the scene.

When the phone rings, the audio returns to normal, signaling the daydream is over.

Dramatic Value

Once you cross the threshold and accept that sound does not need to be rooted in reality, that sound can be pulled from anywhere in expressing a character's thoughts, a huge creative door opens. The example, taken from *Barton Fink*, underscores that sound and picture do not need to match. In fact it's the mismatch that gives the scene heightened interest by suggesting we are hearing Barton's inner thoughts.

Barton Fink (1991)

Screenplay: Joel Coen & Ethan Coen, Feb. 19, 1990.

HIS ROOM

As Barton enters.

The room is small and cheaply furnished. There is a lumpy
bed with a worn-yellow coverlet, an old secretary table, and
a wooden luggage stand.

As Barton crosses the room we follow to reveal a sink and
wash basin, a house telephone on a rickety night stand, and
a window with yellowing sheers looking on an air shaft.

Barton throws his valise onto the bed where it sinks,
jittering. He shrugs off his jacket.

Pips of sweat stand out on Barton's brow. The room is hot.

He walks across the room, switches on an oscillating fan and
struggles to throw open the window. After he strains at it
for a moment, it slides open with a great wrenching sound.

Barton picks up his Underwood and places it on the secretary
table. He gives the machine a casually affectionate pat.

Next to the typewriter are a few sheets of house stationery:
THE HOTEL EARLE: A DAY OR A LIFETIME.

We pan up to a picture in a cheap wooden frame on the wall
above the desk.

A bathing beauty sits on the beach under a cobalt blue sky.
One hand shields her eyes from the sun as she looks out at a
crashing surf.

The sound of the surf mixes up.

BARTON

Looking at the picture

TRACKING IN ON THE PICTURE

The surf mixes up louder. We hear a gull cry.

The sound snaps off with the ring of a telephone.

Chapter Credits By Film Element

35. *Klute* (1971)
Writer:	Andy Lewis (Screenplay)
Writer	David Lewis (Screenplay)
Director:	Alan J. Pakula
Production Company:	Gus Productions
Production Company:	Warner Bros.
Distributor:	Warner Bros.

36. *ET* (1982)
Writer:	Melissa Mathison (Screenplay)
Director:	Steven Spielberg
Production Company:	Amblin Entertainment
Production Company:	Universal Pictures
Distributor:	Columbia TriStar Home Video (USA) (DVD)

37. *Barton Fink* (1991)
Writer:	Joel Coen (Screenplay) &
Writer:	Ethan Coen (Screenplay)
Director:	Joel Coen
Director:	Ethan Coen (Uncredited)
Production Company:	Circle Films Inc.
Production Company:	Working Title Films
Distributor:	20th Century Fox Film Corporation

38. *Barton Fink* (1991)
Same as above.

SECTION 7

MUSIC

39. Film Element: Lyrics as Narrator

The lyrics of a song can act as the voice of a character. They can reveal the inner thoughts in a way that can be more interesting than a simple "talking heads" scene. Lyrics can also be used as the voice of the narrator. Lyrics add another delivery system with which to parcel out character and thematic information. *Apocaplyse Now* offers a powerful example of this.

Film Example: *Apocalypse Now*

Apocalypse Now opens with the Doors' song "The End." The lyrics establish the theme, conflict, and mood of the piece. As the Doors were a band from the period of the Vietnam War, the music serves to anchor the film historically. The nihilistic lyrics immediate set the tone for the audience. This will be a critical view of war. It will show us the underbelly, not the brass and polish. The inverted sense of right and wrong, good and evil in a world gone mad is also suggested by putting a song with lyrics that start with "This is the end" at the beginning of the film. This initial inversion is continually repeated in other forms of the films. The first time we see the protagonist, for example, he is in close-up and upside down — a graphic interpretation of the theme already established by the lyrics.

Dramatic Value

As lyrics are a poetry, they can set up any idea. As thematic songs are sparingly used, the audience will expect the lyrics to be significant. This is especially true when they are placed at the beginning of a film, "the most expensive real-estate" in a movie.

Script Note

The lyrics were not included in the original script by John Milius and Francis Coppola. Writers should note that there have been many movies written around a specific song. However, it's important to get the rights first. All rights are not available and putting copyrighted material in a script is a risk. If the music is only intended as ambience, then stating the kind of music (such as jazz or western, for example) is a better choice.

Other Films

Sea of Love
Play Misty for Me
Blue Velvet
Miller's Crossing ("Danny Boy")

Apocalypse Now (1979) (Page 1)

Screenplay: John Milius and Francis Coppola.

The following page is from a transcript of the movie, not from the original screenplay.

```
The opening scene :


        THE END BY THE DOORS
    This is the end
    Beautiful friend
    This is the end
    My only friend, the end
    Of our elaborate plans, the end
    Of everything that stands, the end
    No safety or surprise, the end
    I'll never look into your eyes...again
    Can you picture what will be
    So limitless and free
    Desperately in need...of some...stranger's hand
    In a...desperate land
    Lost in a romance...wilderness of pain
    And all the children are insane
    All the children are insane
    Waiting for the summer rain, yeah
```

40. Film Element: Symbolic Use of Music

In a stirring scene from *Shawshank Redemption*, we see music symbolically used. It is the turning point for its main character, Red. It isn't the particular selection of music or what the music means that moves Red and the other men in Shawshank prison. It's the idea of music itself.

Film Example: *Shawshank Redemption*

Andy Dufresne is the newly arrived prisoner at Shawshank Prison. Andy soon befriends Red, a longtime inmate. Unlike the other men, Andy will not give up his humanity or his sense of hope. This puts Red at a crossroads: Will he stay on course and become an institutionalized man, or will he take up the new path Andy represents? Up until the mid-point Red has preferred to watch Andy. He's impressed, but doubtful that Andy's philosophy can survive Shawshank.

At the midpoint scene, Andy's hope has paid off. After five years of letter writing, the prison library receives donations of hundreds of records and books. In celebration Andy plays a record in the library. Angered by the guards who scream for him to turn off the music, Andy locks the door. He switches on the P.A. system so the music can be heard through every speaker in the prison. Hearing the music fuels Red's most significant turning point. He knows something inside him has crossed over to the other side, and he can't go back.

Dramatic Value

Here the symbolic use of music acts as a catalyst for change. Structurally it underscores the movie's mid-point.

Other Films

The Piano
Out of Africa

Shawshank Redemption (1994) (Scene 131)

Screenplay: Frank Darabont. Based upon the story "Rita Hayworth and Shawshank Redemption" by Stephen King.

```
131 INT -- GUARD STATION/OUTER OFFICE -- DAY (1955) (Page 131)

------

He slides the Mozart album from its sleeve, lays it on the
platter, and lowers the tone arm to his favorite cut. The
needle HISSES in the groove...and the MUSIC begins, lilting
and gorgeous. Andy sinks into Wiley's chair, overcome by its
beauty.
```

```
145 EXT -- EXERCISE YARD -- DAY (1955) (Page 145)

CAMERA TRACKS along groups of men, all riveted.

                RED (V.O.)
        I have no idea to this day what
        them two Italian ladies were
        singin' about. Truth is, I don't
        want to know. Some things are best
        left unsaid. I like to think they
        were singin' about something so
        beautiful it can't be expressed in
        words, and makes your heart ache
        because of it.

CAMERA brings us to Red.

                RED (V.O.)
        I tell you, those voices soared.
        Higher and farther than anybody in
        a gray place dares to dream. It was
        like some beautiful bird flapped
        into our drab little cage and made
        these walls dissolve away...and for
        the briefest of moments -- every
        last man at Shawshank felt free.
```

(Another exchange occurs between Andy and Red a few weeks later, see scene 150.)

41. Film Element: Music as a Moveable Prop

As in the previous example, music can be used as story element. In *Out of Africa*, as in *Shawshank Redemption*, it is used to express an idea (freedom) which is linked to a specific character. As it is represented by a tangible, moveable prop in *Out of Africa* and appears repeatedly, it can also be used to track changing relationships and values over time.

Film Example: *Out of Africa*

Karen Dinesen, a young Danish woman (Meryl Streep), arrives in Kenya in 1913 to marry a penniless aristocrat for his title. Despite the terrain and arduous journey, she brings crates of china and silver to fill her new home.

Karen's marriage to Bror Blixen is soon over and Karen falls in love with Denys, an American (Robert Redford). Denys gives her a gramophone, symbolizing their friendship and the freedom he represents.

First Use
When Denys first gives Karen the gramophone she views the gesture cynically, suggesting that Denys is trying to seduce her. Denys is mildly insulted, and indicates that, quite the contrary, it's a gift between friends (page 74) .

Second Use
Ten pages later when Karen confides to a friend that all is not well in her new life, Denys' presence in her marriage is represented by the gramophone playing softly behind them (page 85).

Final Use
In the final scenes of the movie we see Karen has transformed. The guarded, class-conscious Dane now dances with her lover barefoot on the grass under the night sky. She has lost all her material wealth. This time the gramophone provides the music for their dance, rather than underscoring her unresolved troubles (page 126) .

Dramatic Value

Once the symbol is set up, each subsequent reference can suggest change.

Out of Africa (1985)

Screenplay: Kurt Luedke, Aug. 1983. See Chapter Credits.

First Use (Page 74–75)

EXT. IN THE FOREST DAY-DAY

She's riding home, Ismail walking beside her with her rifle.
Now faint, the SOUND of a Mozart sympathy (O.S.). Puzzled,
she strains to hear, puts her horse to a trot, leaving
Ismail behind.

EXT. THE TERRACE-DAY

Denys's safari truck, with Kanuthia and Wasili. He's on the
terrace with champagne, gramophone blaring.

> DENYS
> (reduces the volume)
>
> I thought you'd like some music.
> I got another for myself.

1.

Second Use (Page 85)

INT. DINING ROOM-NIGHT

GRAMOPHONE MUSIC, low. They're in evening clothes. He's
flushed, perspiring. Juma clears the plates.

> KAREN
> (cheerful)
>
> I'm in the worst sort of trouble now.
>
> BERKELEY
>
> Denys?--

2.

Third Use (Page 126)

EXT. THE TERRACE-NIGHT

Denys brings the gramophone to the old stone mill table.
They wind it, start the record: a WALTZ, made for an
eighteenth century ballroom. She takes off her shoes.

3.

Chapter Credits By Film Element

39. *Apocalypse Now* (1979)
Writer: John Milius (Screenplay) &
Writer: Francis Coppola (Screenplay)
Writer: Joseph Conrad (Uncredited)
Director: Francis Coppola
Production Company: Zoetrope
Distributor: United Artists

40. *Shawshank Redemption* (1994)
Writer: Frank Darabont (Screenplay)
Writer: Stephen King (Short Story: "Rita Hayworth and
                                Shawshank Redemption")
Director: Frank Darabont
Production Company: Castle Rock Entertainment
Production Company   Columbia Pictures Corporation
Distributor: Columbia Pictures
Distributor: Columbia TriStar (USA)

41. *Out of Africa* (1985)
Writer: Kurt Luedtke (Screenplay)
Writer: Isak Dinesen (Memoirs)
Writer: A.E. Housman (Poem: "To an Athlete, Dying Young")
                                (Uncredited))
Writer: Errol Trzebinski (Book: *Silence will Speak*)
Director: Sydney Pollack
Production Company: Mirage Entertainment
Distributor: MCA/Universal Pictures

SECTION **8**

SCENE
TRANSITIONS

SECTION 8: SCENE TRANSITIONS (AUDIO AND VISUAL)

The moment between the end of one scene and the beginning of another is called a transition. Each transition presents the writer and director with an opportunity to convey story information by virtue of how the scenes are cut together. The scenes can simply be cut with no intentional reference or constructed to add a story element.

A matching transition is one way to exploit this opportunity and can be achieved in an infinite number of ways. Essentially, a matching transition "matches" the outgoing shot with the incoming shot. This can also be done with sound.

Visual Match-Cut

A match-cut generally refers to picture. Two images can be match-cut based on similarity of content, graphics, shape, motion, size, graphics, or color, for example. Take a look on page 249 where you can see an incredible match-cut based on similarity of shape from *Dolores Claiborne*. Match-cuts are used to move the story along, creating a new idea based on the juxtaposition of two images. Dissolves between images, instead of a hard cut, can also be used.

Matching Audio Segue

Although the term "matching audio segue" is not a standard sound term, we'll use it for the sake of simplicity when referring to an audio effect analogous to a visual match cut. In the case of audio, then, a "matching audio segue" occurs when two similar or matching sounds are heard, one after another, creating an unexpected inference. This is similar to the effect of a visual match-cut. Often in the case of audio the outgoing sound will be laid over the incoming sound. The outgoing sound will fade out as the incoming sound takes over, the effect is much like a matching visual dissolve.

Audio Bridge

An audio bridge works in a completely different manner. Here you have an outgoing sound from one scene that continues over a new image or shot. An audio bridge is when one sound is used to connect two shots or two scenes together aurally.

Suggested Reading

One of the best discussions on transitions is made in Margaret Mehring's book entitled *Screenwriting*.

Film Elements

Audio

42. Matching Audio Segue   *Sorry, Wrong Number; Fatal Attraction*

43. Audio Bridge (dialog)   *Citizen Kane*

44. Audio Bridge (sound effects)   *Barton Fink*

Visual

45. Visual Match-Cut — Graphic Similarity   *Single White Female*

46. Visual Match-Cut — Pattern & Color   *Citizen Kane*

47. Visual Match-Cut — Action   *2001: A Space Odyssey*

48. Visual Match-Cut — Idea   *Requiem for a Dream*

49. Visual Match-Cut — Idea   *Harold and Maude*

50. Extended Match-Dissolve — Time Transition   *Titanic* (double match-dissolve)

51. Disrupted Match-Cut   *Bound*

42. Film Element: Matching Audio Segue

A *matching audio segue* occurs when one source of audio fades out, while another matching audio source fades in. This occurs between scenes or within a scene. Matching audio segues have been put to some ingenious uses. Here is one kind put to two different uses.

Film Example: *Sorry, Wrong Number*

By Act Three we know that Leona Stevenson (Barbara Stanwyck) is about to be murdered. Earlier, we have seen a screeching subway train pass by her window every night at the same time. When the murderer enters her room and reaches his hands to her neck, the screeching train passes at its usual time inadvertently covering Stanwyk's scream. By the time the train passes, she is dead.

Film Example: *Fatal Attraction*

We see a similar use in *Fatal Attraction*. Just before the climax scene Dan (Michael Douglas) is downstairs making tea for his wife. His wife is recovering from a near fatal accident caused by Eve, Dan's lover (Glen Close). As Dan's wife runs a bath upstairs, Eve suddenly appears holding a knife.

Just as Eve attacks Dan's wife, the tea kettle whistles. Unable to hear his wife's screams Dan walks slowly over to the kettle. Meanwhile we cut back upstairs where his wife fights for her life. When Dan finally removes the kettle from the burner, he hears something, but at first he's disoriented. He can't make out what he's hearing. Finally, after a suspenseful beat, he deciphers the sound and races upstairs. In this case, the masking sound (the tea kettle) is silenced — *just in time*.

Dramatic Value

In both films sound is used to mask an important event. In *Fatal Attraction* the tea kettle masks a woman's screams and in *Sorry, Wrong Number* a roaring train overpowers the cries of a woman about to be murdered.

Sorry, Wrong Number (1948)

Radio Play: Lucille Fletcher; Play: Lucille Fletcher ;
Screenplay: Lucille Fletcher.

Excerpt below is from *Sorry, Wrong Number* (the play).

Final Scene:

Scene: We see on the dark c. stage, the shadow of
door opening.

Screaming: The Police!

Scene: On stage, swift rush of a shadow, advancing
to bed--sound of her voice is choked out, as

Operator: Ringing the Police Department.

Phone is rung. We hear the sound of a train
beginning to fade in. On second ring, Mrs.
Stevenson screams again, but the roaring of train
drowns out her voice. For a few seconds, we hear
nothing but roaring of train, then dying away.

The scene continues.

1.

2.

Sorry, Wrong Number   3.

1.

2.

Fatal Attraction   3.

43. Film Element: Audio Bridge (Dialog)

An *Audio Bridge* is when two scenes are connected by a single audio source. In this case it's done with dialog.

Film Example: *Citizen Kane*

In an incredible use of an audio bridge, twenty years of time is compressed with a single line of dialog.

Shot 1
Young Kane is seated on the floor opening Christmas presents. The young boy looks up at his guardian and says, "Merry Christmas."

Shot 2
We then cut to a new image as Kane's guardian completes his greeting saying "and a Happy New Year." In the new image Thatcher is now twenty years older.

Dramatic Value

Compression of Time.

AUDIO BRIDGE

44. Film Element: Audio Bridge (Sound Effects)

As explained in the previous example, an audio bridge links two scenes with a single audio source. In the preceding example from *Citizen Kane*, a dialog bridge was used to flashforward.

One of the most famous uses occurs in the opening scenes of *Apocalypse Now*. Here the sound of helicopter blades is laid over the image of the spinning blades of a fan. This simple but ingenious sound bridge designed by legendary sound editor Walter Murch takes us inside Captain Willard's mind. Through the use of the sound bridge we believe we hear what he is hearing.

In an entirely different use, going the opposite direction, the offscreen sound of typing is heard first and connected to the onscreen source in the adjacent scene. In this example, taken from *Barton Fink*, the sound bridge suggests continuity of time.

Film Example: *Barton Fink*

We track in down the hallway of Barton Fink's hotel.

Shot 1

As we track down the hallway of the hotel we see men's shoes stationed in front of every door. The only sound, however, comes from Barton's room — that of typing. The sound of typing effectively differentiates Barton from the other residents.

Shot 2

When we cut inside the room, the rhythm of the typing continues uninterrupted suggesting real time. The shot is Barton's POV of keys striking the page.

Dramatic Value

The long tracking shot down the hallway, coupled with the unbroken rhythm of the typing, suggests that Barton has finally found the story for his script. Rather than tell us on the dialog track, the audience is asked to participate in the scene by figuring out what the sound effects mean. This makes the scene more dramatic, challenging, and memorable for the viewer.

Barton Fink (1991) (Scene 9-10, Page 19)

Screenplay: Joel Coen & Ethan Coen, Feb. 19, 1990.

TRACKING SHOT

We are in the sixth-floor hallway of the Earle, late at night. A pair of shoes sits before each door. Faintly, from one of the rooms, we can hear the clack. clack. clack. of a typewriter.

It grows louder as we track forward.

EXTREME CLOSE SHOT - TYPEWRITER

Close on the typing so that we see only each letter as it is typed, without context.

One by one the letters clack on: a-u-d-i-b-l-e. After a short beat, a period strikes.

1.

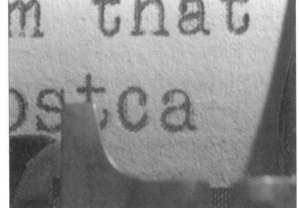

2.

45. Film Element: Visual Match-Cut (Graphic Similarity)

A *visual match-cut* is achieved when the image at the end of one scene "matches" the incoming image of the next scene. The edit can be a "cut" or a "dissolve." For the sake of simplicity the term "cut" will be used throughout.

A visual match-cut can suggest similarity or contrast. It can, for example, externalize ideas about theme, motivation, or the passage of time. In *Single White Female* it's used to tell us about location.

Film Example: *Single White Female*

The protagonist in *Single White Female* (Bridget Fonda) lives with her boyfriend in a N.Y. apartment house. Soon after the movie begins, the couple fight.

Shot 1
As the two argue, the camera cuts to an ornate wrought iron grill covering a nearby heating vent.

Shot 2
The film then match-cuts to an *almost* identical grill. Because of the unique pattern we assume it must belong to a neighboring apartment. Then the camera pulls back to reveal the protagonist's "trusted" neighbor listening to the argument through the vent.

Dramatic Value

By match-cutting the two grills, the neighbor's location is immediately established. The director could have cut outside to an exterior shot, then an interior hallway shot, then cut inside — but it would have cost a lot of shots. By match-cutting, it takes only one shot to establish that we are in the same building. By having the neighbor lean in to listen, we learn about the neighbor and also find ourselves leaning in to eavesdrop. In this case the match-cut is used for economy, reveals the neighbor's character, and emphasizes to the audience the importance of the couple's dialog.

Script Note

In the excerpted match-cut, the order of match was reversed. In the script we go from the neighbor's apartment to Allie's. In the film we start with Allie's grill and then cut to her neighbor's.

Single White Female (1992) (Scene 3-4)

Screenplay: Don Roos, Draft: August 9, 1991. Based on *S.W.F. Seeks Same* by John Lutz.

3. INT. GRAHAM'S APARTMENT - GRAHAM'S BEDROOM - NIGHT

THE SOUNDS OF SEX ARE LOUDER. We've seen this shot before. The CAMERA MOVES DOWN THE BEDROOM WALL, across the floor, past shoes, socks, underwear, rumpled bedclothes, to GRAHAM KNOX, thirty-eight. He's in bed. A book has fallen open in his lap; his cat, Carmen, sleeps at his feet. He's listening uncomfortably, straining towards:

AN AIR VENT

Which carries the SOUNDS OF SEX from an apartment below...

4. INT. ALLIE'S APARTMENT - ALLIE'S BEDROOM - NIGHT

The sex is here, and the Eartha Kitt. We MOVE from the air vent past a small teddy bear on the floor, a night light, a lamp covered with a silk scarf, finally to the bed where SAM RAWSON is making love to ALLIE JONES. ---

1.

2.

3.

46. Film Element: Visual Match-Cut (Pattern and Color)

Like a dissolve, *match-cutting* on *color* can smooth out a cut. A great match-cut can work both on a story level and aesthetically. Here's how an intricate black-and-white pattern was match-cut in *Citizen Kane*.

Film Example: *Citizen Kane*

This match-cut, taken from Act One of *Citizen Kane*, works on a number of story levels.

The outgoing shot depicts lead journalist, Thompson, reading Thatcher's diary for clues about Kane's life.

Shot 1

The first shot is a POV shot of the diary page that Thompson is reading. The page is white with black handwriting. This shot is cut with an almost identically patterned image.

Shot 2

The second shot or incoming shot is also predominantly white with small flecks of black, mimicking Thatcher's handwriting.

A closer look reveals the white is snow and the flecks of black, a small child playing with his sled. It's as though the content described by the handwriting is actually embedded in the lettering. When the dissolve occurs, the content emerges out of the handwriting, suggesting a link between the two.

Dramatic Value

Here the match-cut transforms text into image suggesting that text graphics and content are inherently linked.

Citizen Kane (1941)

Screenplay: Herman J. Mankiewicz and Orson Welles.

Int. Thatcher Memorial Library--Day--1940

The camera has not held on the entire page. It has been following the words with the same action that the eye does in reading. On the last words, the white page of the paper

Dissolves into

Ext. Mrs. Kane's Boarding house--Day--1870

The white of a great field of snow--(seen from the angle of parlor window). In the same position as the last word in above Insert, appears the tiny figure of CHARLES FOSTER KANE, aged five, (almost like an animated cartoon.) He is in the act of throwing a snowball at the camera. It sails toward us and over our heads, out of scene.

Reverse angle--on the house featuring a large sign reading:

MRS. KANE'S BOARDINGHOUSE
HIGH CLASS MEALS AND LODGING
INQUIRE WITHIN

CHARLES KANE'S snowball hits the sign.

1.

2.

3.

47. Film Element: Visual Match-Cut (Action)

A *match-cut on action* means that the visuals of one scene are matched with the visuals in the next through similarity of action. In this case the match-cut on action conveys time compression.

Film Example: *2001: A Space Odyssey*

2001: A Space Odyssey opens with a spectacular sequence depicting the evolutionary stages of mankind.

Shot 1

The last image of the sequence shows a prehistoric man toss a bone into the air.

Shot 2

The spinning bone (action) is matched in the next scene with a moving space ship (action).

In a single match-cut we travel from prehistoric man to the space era. It's a spectacular use of a match-cut on action.

Dramatic Value

Time compression through a flashforward that is achieved through a match-cut on action.

Other Films

All That Jazz. By cutting on action several dancers are made to appear as one. Each new dancer is shot alone on stage auditioning. Each cut shows a new dancer in exactly the same spot and continuing the motion of the previous dancer. Here the match-cut on action suggests both the passage of time and the interchangeability of dancers.

48. Film Element: Visual Match-Cut (Idea)

A *cut on idea* is when two shots are cut together and, by their juxtaposition, a third idea is suggested. This new idea is the sum of the first two.

Film Example: *Requiem for a Dream*

In *Requiem for a Dream*, Sara (Ellen Burstyn), a middle-aged woman, lives and breathes bad TV. Then one day, she believes she's been invited to be on a television show. Sara starts popping pills to lose weight. The pills do terrible things to her. Her doctor is too busy too help her, consequently she finds herself in an endless hallucination.

Shot 1

At the end of this first hallucination Sara walks into a close-up. The fish eye lens warps her face. We hold on it for a moment, then cut to a matching close-up of Tyrone, a young drug addict and friend of Sara's son.

Shot 2

Tyrone's close-up is taken with a normal lens straight on. He stands behind jail cell bars.

Dramatic Value

The cut suggests that Sara and Tyrone are united by drugs, each in their own prison. We subconsciously apply the jail bars to both characters. We derive the new meaning from the ideas suggested by the juxtaposition.

Other Films

Klute

49. Film Element: Visual Match-Cut (Idea)

As in the previous example a *match cut on idea* is when two images placed side by side suggest a new idea. The new idea is not inherently obvious in either image when viewed separately. In the previous example it was used to link two characters. In this case the cut visually answers a specific question.

Film Example: *Harold and Maude*

Harold is a young man who attempts to free himself and escape his mother's values. After staging countless suicide attempts, he is sent to a psychiatrist.

Shot 1 (See Script Excerpt)
The cut on idea is in response to the psychiatrist's question, "How do you feel about your mother?"

Shot 2 (See Script Excerpt)
The question is answered visually by an insert shot of the giant steel wrecking ball.

Script Note

In the movie, Maude, not the psychiatrist, asks the question and the insert shot answers her.

Dramatic Value

The audience forms their own idea through the juxtaposition of shots. Rather than learn Harold's view through dialog, Harold's answer comes in the form of a visual metaphor.

Harold and Maude (1971) Scene 12-13, Pages 4-5)

Screenplay: Colin Higgins, 1971.

```
12. INT. PSYCHIATRIST'S OFFICE - DAY

----

Harold is lying on a couch, perfectly relaxed. The PSYCHIATRIST,
less so, is seated by him.

                    PSYCHIATRIST

              ---
              How do you feel about your mother?

13. INSERT - STOCK

A giant steel ball on a demolition crane crashes into a brick
wall collapsing it with much noise and dust.
```

1.

2.

3.

4.

50. Film Element: Extended Match Dissolve (Time Transition)

A visual match can be joined with a cut or dissolve. A dissolve fades out one image as the next image fades in. This gives the transition a certain smoothness.

Film Example: *Titanic*

In a fascinating "double match-dissolve" director James Cameron takes us from the charcoal drawing of protagonist Rose (Kate Winslet) to her close-up as a young woman.

Then, using a close-up of her eye as a new starting point, Cameron starts a second series of match dissolves. Through the second set of dissolves, we see Rose transform from a woman of twenty to a woman of 100.

Dramatic Value

The long dissolves smooth the cut between images, making the aging process and time transition feel seamless and organic.

Script Note

In the script the two dissolves are separated. In the film they are cut back-to-back.

Titanic (1997) (Scene 67, Page 41)

Screenplay: James Cameron, May 7, 1996, Revised.

*Cal has just given Rose 'Le coeur de mer' diamond and then—We
jump in, mid-scene.*

```
67 INT. ROSE'S BEDROOM - NIGHT

-----

He gazes at the image of the two of them in the mirror.

                    CAL
          It's for royalty. And we are royalty.

His fingers caress her neck and throat. He seems himself to be
disarmed by Rose's elegance and beauty. His emotion is, for
the first time, unguarded.

                    CAL
          There's nothing I couldn't give you. There's
          nothing I'd deny you if you would deny me. Open
          your heart to me, Rose.

CAMERA begins to TRACK IN ON ROSE. Closer and closer, during
the following:

                    OLD ROSE (V.O.)
          Of course his gift was only to reflect light back
          onto himself, to illuminate the greatness that
          was Caledon Hockley. It was a cold stone... a
          heart of ice.

Finally, when Rose's eyes FILL FRAME, we MORPH SLOWLY to
her eyes as the are now... transforming through 84 years of
life...

                    TRANSITION

68 INT. KELDYSH IMAGING SHACK

Without a cut the wrinkled, weathered landscape of age has
appeared around her eyes. But the eyes themselves are the
same.

                    OLD ROSE
          After all these years, feel it closing around my
          throat like a dog collar.

THE CAMERA PUllS BACK to show her whole face.
```

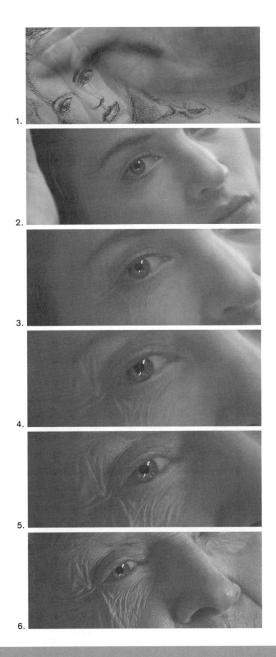

1.

2.

3.

4.

5.

6.

51. Film Element: Disrupted Match-Cut

A *disrupted match-cut* occurs when two matched images are separated by a single shot. Interestingly, little associative power is lost by the middle shot. When the images of the outer shots visually rhyme, the audience will continue to forge a link between the two.

Film Example: *Bound*

Corky (Gina Gershon), a young woman just out of jail, has taken a "straight" job as a general contractor in a mob-owned building. In the elevator she meets and is immediately attracted to Violet (Jennifer Tilly), who lives with a mobster next door.

A few hours later, while Corky works on the plumbing, the sound of a man screaming comes from the mobster's condo next door. Here's how the disrupted match cut appears in the film.

Shot 1
Corky works in the apartment next door. She hears the sound of a man screaming. She stares at the toilet bowl. It is as though the sound is coming up through the toilet.

Shot 2
A brief reaction shot of Corky listening. Corky looks back down again.

Shot 3
The water in the toilet bowl begins to move. Suddenly blood sprays onto the water's surface.

This third shot first appears to be in Corky's apartment. In reality it's taken from the mobster's bathroom. When we cut to a wider shot we see a man hunched over the toilet bowl being severely beaten.

Dramatic Value

Like the match-cut in *Single White Female*, this cut takes us from one location to another. In this case, the blood falling in the toilet disorients the audience temporarily. When we cut to a wider shot, our questions are answered. It has also prepared us for the brutality.

Script Note

The film places Corky's reaction shot between the match-cuts. In this version of the script, it's a straight match-cut.

Other Films

Single White Female

Bound (1996) (Page 31)

Screenplay: Larry Wachowski & Andy Wachowski, First Draft, Sept. 28, 1994.

We cut into the end of the scene:

```
INT. BATHROOM

---

We begin to close in on Corky as she listens to each thud, watching
something that disturbs her.

                    ANGRY VOICE
          You shit! You piece of shit!

With each thud the water in the toilet shimmers like a struck drum
cymbal. As we move closer the sound swells until--

MATCH CUT TO:

INT. CEASAR'S BATHROOM

Where blood splatters the toilet, heavy drops hitting the water and
spreading like inverted mushroom clouds.

                    ANGRY VOICE
          Did that hurt? News flash fucko: I'm just getting started.
```

1.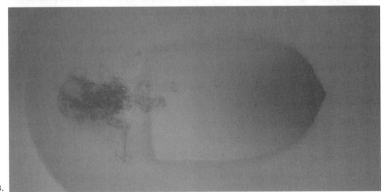

2.

3.

Chapter Credits By Film Element

42. *Sorry, Wrong Number* (1948)
Writer: Lucille Fletcher (Screenplay)
Writer: Lucille Fletcher (Play) (Formerly a Radio Play)
Director: Anatole Litvak
Production Company: Hal Wallis Productions
Production Company: Paramount Pictures
Distributor: Paramount Pictures

43. *Citizen Kane* (1941)
Writer: Herman J. Mankiewicz (Screenplay) &
Writer: Orson Welles (Screenplay)
Writer: John Houseman (Screenplay) (Uncredited)
Director: Orson Welles
Production Company: Mercury Productions
Production Company: RKO Pictures
Distributor: RKO Pictures Inc. (1941) USA Theatrical
Distributor: Warner Home Video (DVD)

44. *Barton Fink* (1991)
Writer: Joel Coen (Screenplay) &
Writer: Ethan Coen (Screenplay)
Director: Joel Coen
Director: Ethan Coen (Uncredited)
Production Company: Circle Films Inc.
Production Company: Working Title Films
Distributor: 20th Century Fox Film Corporation

45. *Single White Female* (1992)
Writer: Don Roos (Screenplay)
Writer: John Lutz (Novel: *SWF seeks same*)
Director: Barbet Shroeder
Production Company: Columbia Pictures
Distributor: Columbia Pictures

46. *Citizen Kane* (1941)
Writer: Herman J. Mankiewicz (Screenplay) &
Writer: Orson Welles (Screenplay)
Writer: John Houseman (Screenplay) (Uncredited)
Director: Orson Welles
Production Company: Mercury Productions
Production Company: RKO Pictures
Distributor: RKO Pictures Inc. (1941) USA Theatrical
Distributor: Warner Home Video (DVD)

47. *2001: A Space Odyssey* (1968)
Writer: Stanley Kubrick (Screenplay) &
Writer: Arthur C. Clarke (Screenplay)
Writer: Arthur C. Clarke (Story: *The Sentinel*)
Director: Stanley Kubrick
Production Company: MGM
Production Company: Polaris
Distributor: Criterion Collection/MGM

48. *Requiem for A Dream* (2000)
Writer: Hubert Selby Jr. (Screenplay) and
Writer: Darren Aronofsky (Screenplay)
Writer: Hubert Sclby Jr. (Novel)
Director: Darren Aronofsky
Production Company: Artisan Entertainment
Production Company: Bandeira Entertainment
Production Company: Industry Entertainment
Production Company: Protozoa Pictures
Production Company   Requiem for a Dream
Production Company: Sibling Productions
Production Company: Thousand Words
Production Company: Truth and Soul
Distributor: Artisan Entertainment

49. *Harold and Maude* (1971)
Writer: Colin Higgins (Screenplay)
Director: Hal Ashby
Production Company: Paramount Pictures
Distributor: Paramount Pictures

50. *Titanic* (1997)
Writer: James Cameron
Director: James Cameron
Production Company: 20th Century Fox
Production Company: Lightstorm Entertainment
Production Company: Paramount Pictures
Distributor: 20th Century Fox

51. *Bound* (1996)
Writer: The Wachowski Brothers & The Wachowski Brothers
Director: The Wachowski Brothers & The Wachowski Brothers
Production Company: Dino de Laurentiis Productions
Production Company: Spelling Films
Distributor: Gramercy Pictures

SECTION **9**

CAMERA
LENSES

52. Film Element: Wide-Angle

One of the qualities of a wide-angle lens is its ability to deliver great depth-of-field to an image. This means that objects in the foreground, middleground, and background can be in focus simultaneously. This enables action to be staged in-depth. In the following scene from *Citizen Kane*, the action is staged along three different horizontal planes — all of which can be clearly viewed by the audience at the same time.

Film Example: *Citizen Kane*

In this first flashback sequence in *Citizen Kane*, each character is stationed along the z-axis on a different horizontal plane.

Three Planes

1. Inside and in the foreground Kane's mother signs documents forfeiting her paternal rights.

2. In the middleground her husband looks on angrily.

3. Outside and in the background, Kane plays in the snow literally placed outside the decision making.

Dramatic Value

By exploiting the depth-of-field of the lens, each character can inhabit their own horizontal plane. In this way characters can be staged in-depth. This allows the audience to see each character reacting to one event simultaneously and in real time.

Script Note

Although the staging in the film was slightly different than the script, the script excerpt is included to show writers how the camera movement was described.

Citizen Kane (1941)

Screenplay: Herman J. Mankiewicz and Orson Welles.

```
INT. PARLOR - MRS. KANE'S BOARDINGHOUSE - DAY - 1870
```

Camera is angling through the window, but the window-frame is not cut into scene. We see only the field of snow again, same angle as in previous scene. Charles is manufacturing another snowball. Now -

Camera pulls back, the frame of the window appearing, and we are inside the parlor of the boardinghouse. Mrs. Kane, aged about 28, is looking out towards her son. Just as we take her in she speaks:

> MRS. KANE
> (calling out)

Be careful, Charles!

> THATCHER'S VOICE

Mrs. Kane -

> MRS. KANE
> (calling out the window
> almost on top of this)

Pull your muffler around your neck,
Charles -

But Charles, deliriously happy in the snow, is oblivious to this and is running away. Mrs. Kane turns into camera and we see her face - a strong face, worn and kind.

> THATCHER'S VOICE

I think we'll have to tell him now -

Camera now pulls back further, showing Thatcher standing before a table on which is his stove-pipe hat and an imposing multiplicity of official-looking documents. He is 26 and, as might be expected, a very stuffy young man, already very expensive and conservative looking, even in Colorado.

> MRS. KANE

I'll sign those papers -

> KANE SR.

You people seem to forget that I'm
the boy's father.

At the sound of Kane Sr.'s voice, both have turned to him and the camera pulls back still further, taking him in.

Kane Sr., who is the assistant curator in a livery stable, has been groomed as elegantly as is likely for this meeting ever since daybreak.

From outside the window can be heard faintly the wild and cheerful cries of the boy, blissfully cavorting in the snow.

53. Film Element: Wide-Angle (Vistas and Establishing Shots)

In addition to having great use in deep-focus interior shots, the wide-angle lens is also naturally suited for exterior establishing shots. Its ability to record wide vista shots makes it invaluable in establishing exterior locations.

In Jane Campion's *The Piano*, the wide-angle is used to capture the New Zealand coastline. However, as in many other scenes, Campion doubles-up the storytelling job of the lens.

Campion shows the changing relationship of her characters by positioning them along the wide vista that the lens can record. In this way the lens records the image, but is also put to work to advance the story.

Film Example: *The Piano*

In this scene, the protagonist, Ada (Holly Hunter), has convinced a local resident (Harvey Keitel) to take her to her piano left on the beach. When we first see the two on the beach, Keitel takes up the far left side of the frame, and Hunter the right. The wide vista shot is able to place a huge distance between them, mirroring the state of their relationship. By the end of the scene, however, we understand that the relationship has changed. Keitel travels toward Hunter, closing the gap between them with each step.

Dramatic Value

By coding the distance between two characters, and its opposite, proximity, the wide-angle lens can suggest emotional changes pictorially.

The Piano (1993) (Scene 29-31)

Screenplay: Jane Campion, 4th Draft 1991.

Sc 29   EXT   BEACH   DAY

The sky is blue with long wisps of cloud.

The party of three break onto the long expanse of beach
where the piano still stands. It has not been without
visitors. There are footprints on the sand and some of the
boards have been pulled back.

ADA passes BAINES, walking urgently towards it. Soon,
ADA has removed enough boards that she may lift the lid
and play the keys. BAINES stays back. ADA takes great
delight in feeling her fingers on the keys again. Her whole
composition is altered. She is animated, joyful,excited.

Down on the wet sand FLORA does a wild dance of her own
invention using a seaweed wig. She finishes by rolling down
the beach in the sand.

BAINES views them with suspicion, yet he is magnetically
drawn to the spectacle. He has never seen women behave with
so much abandon. His attention fixes on ADA's uninhibited
emotional playing, and as he watches, he finds himself
edging irresistibly closer.

Sc 30   EXT   BEACH   LATE AFTER NOON

The shadows are long on the sand when BAINES collects the
boards. ADA and FLORA are attempting a duet. ADA notices
him come towards them with the boards, obviously intending
that they should leave. Her mood darkens, she continues
playing stubbornly even though FLORA has stopped. Abruptly
she finishes. In black spirits she replaces her cape and
bonnet. BAINES is struck by this sudden change, he watches
her mesmerised as he replaces the boards.

1.

2.

54. Film Element: Telephoto

A *telephoto lens* has attributes opposite to those of the wide-angle lens. The telephoto brings distant objects closer to the viewer. It compresses space, making objects appear to be on the same horizontal plane. Its shallow depth-of-field throws objects, both in front of and behind the focal point, out of focus.

A wide-angle lens will make any movement toward or away from the camera seem exaggerated. A person running toward the camera will arrive more quickly than expected. This is opposite of the telephoto, where the person will appear to be running on the spot. This quality was exploited to increase suspense in the following scene from *The Graduate*.

Film Example: *The Graduate*

In the final sequence of *The Graduate*, Ben (Dustin Hoffman) races against the clock. He rushes on foot toward the church where his girlfriend is about to be married. By using a telephoto lens, Hoffman's advance toward the camera doesn't seem to net him any gain. Despite his strenuous efforts, he appears to be running on the spot. Because he races against the clock, this greatly adds to the suspense. We are sure he will never make it in time.

Dramatic Value

When a character runs along the z-axis toward the audience their motion will appear slowed down when shot with a telephoto, and speeded up when shot with a wide-angle. The telephoto lens compresses the focal length, thereby making objects that are separated in reality appear on the same horizontal plane. This is the quality, unique to a telephoto lens, that was exploited to heighten suspense.

55. Film Element: Fisheye

Wide-angle lenses are characterized by their short focal lengths. The shorter the focal length, the more the linear distortion. As a fisheye lens is an extreme wide-angle, it creates an exaggerated linear distortion: Its effect is like looking into a mirrored glass ball. *Requiem for a Dream* effectively exploits this characteristic to represent a drug hallucination.

Film Example: *Requiem For A Dream*

Requiem for a Dream follows four drug-addicted characters as they spiral deeper into their addiction. Sara, a middle-aged woman (Ellen Burstyn) pops diet pills believing she is going to be on TV. The television is central to her house-bound life and being on television, the ultimate fantasy.

Hallucination 1 (Watching TV)
Sara's first full-blown hallucination occurs while watching TV. Sara imagines herself on the game show. As Sara's hallucination begins, the camera switches from a wide-angle to a fisheye lens.

The fisheye's natural distortion externalizes Sara's inner turmoil. But what makes this scene brilliant is that the fisheye also mimics the curvature of the television screen. It is as though Sara now lives inside the TV looking out through its curved screen.

A few scenes later Sara appears at her doctor's office seeking help.

Hallucination 2 (Doctor's Office)
The entire doctor's office scene is shot with a fisheye lens. Sara now sees life entirely through the curve of the television screen. She tries to return to normalcy, but the doctor just extends the prescription that is causing her problems.

In her final scene in the movie, her transformation is complete; she no longer fights her hallucinations. She lives within a televised dream and is finally happy.

Dramatic Value

The curvature of the fisheye mimics the central anchor in the character's life, the television screen. In referring back to the television in rendering the hallucination, the choice of lens deepens the story.

Other Films

In Cold Blood

1.

2.

3.

4.

5. Sara Goldfarb, Brooklyn, NY

6.

56. Film Element: Prop Lenses within the Scene (Fisheye)

When a camera films a scene it transfers the photographic properties of the lens to the entire scene. There are, however, ways to include more than one "lens" in a shot. This is by placing reflective objects, with curvatures different than the shooting lens, in the scene. We might think of these objects as "prop lenses," props that change the photographic quality within a limited section of the frame. In a well-known scene from *Citizen Kane* we see such a "prop lens" in action.

Film Example: *Citizen Kane*

As Charles Kane dies in the opening moments of the prologue, he drops a children's novelty item, a small glass ball. The ball crashes to the floor but a large section of the outer shell remains intact. The curvature of the reflective shell creates a second lens in the frame, in this case a fisheye lens. In the next shot the "fisheye" lens dominates the bottom two-thirds of the frame. The rest of the frame portrays the properties of the shooting lens, a wide-angle with comparably little distortion. The fisheye reflects back to us the incoming nurse. Notice the distorted lines of the rectangular doorway.

Dramatic Value

The child's glass ball is the last object that Kane actually sees before dying. And the image is distorted. When Kane drops the ball, he closes his eyes. It is as though his last conscious thoughts are transferred onto the ball. It's as though he mixes the sound of the nurse's footsteps with the fisheye imagery he has just seen. The "prop lens" projects what might be the last images that Kane imagines before dying.

Citizen Kane (1941) (Page 4)

Screenplay: Herman J. Mankiewicz and Orson Welles.

INT. KANE'S BEDROOM - FAINT DAWN - 1940

A snow scene. An incredible one. Big, impossible flakes of
snow, a too picturesque farmhouse and a snow man. The jingling
of sleigh bells in the musical score now makes an ironic
reference to Indian Temple bells - the music freezes -

                         KANE'S OLD OLD VOICE
         Rosebud...

The camera pulls back, showing the whole scene to be contained
in one of those glass balls which are sold in novelty stores
all over the world. A hand - Kane's hand, which has been
holding the ball, relaxes. The ball falls out of his hand and
bounds down two carpeted steps leading to the bed, the camera
following. The ball falls off the last step onto the marble
floor where it breaks, the fragments glittering in the first
rays of the morning sun. This ray cuts an angular pattern
across the floor, suddenly crossed with a thousand bars of
light as the blinds are pulled across the window.

The foot of Kane's bed. The camera very close. Outlined
against the shuttered window, we can see a form - the form of
a nurse, as she pulls the sheet up over his head. The camera
follows this action up the length of the bed and arrives at
the face after the sheet has covered it.

57. Film Element: Objects

When a camera shoots *through* objects like stained glass, water or plastic, for example, it alters the photographic properties of the image. Great creative opportunities have evolved from this. Here's one example taken from *Dances with Wolves*.

Film Example: *Dances with Wolves*

Lieutenant John J. Dunbar has arrived at Fort Sedgewick at the edge of the frontier. This is sometime in 1862. Dunbar's purpose is to see the frontier before it's gone. He meets Major Fambrough at the threshold, who has already gone mad.

After a bizarre first encounter with the Major, Dunbar exits heading out on his journey. While still inside, the Major raises a glass to Dunbar as he looks through the window. We then cut to the Major's POV shot.

What's wonderful about the POV shot is that the Major looks out through the thick, syrupy window panes of his time. The distorted panes add historical authority to the shot. More importantly, the visual distortion created by the window externalizes the Major's own distorted view of reality. A moment later, the Major puts a gun to his head and shoots himself dead.

Dramatic Value

The shot helps to reveal character and foreshadow events.

The thick window pane is an object that would naturally be in the scene. By using its properties creatively, the resulting distorted view doesn't feel false. It feels organic to the scene and is able to do triple duty: convey the events of the scene, reveal character subliminally, and anchor the scene historically.

Other Films

Three Women (shooting through a fish tank)

Bound (shooting through a curved peephole)

Chapter Credits By Film Element

52. *Citizen Kane* (1941)
Writer:	Herman J. Mankiewicz (Screenplay) &
Writer:	Orson Welles (Screenplay)
Writer:	John Houseman (Screenplay) (Uncredited)
Director:	Orson Welles
Production Company:	Mercury Productions
Production Company:	RKO Pictures
Distributor:	RKO Pictures Inc. (1941) USA Theatrical
Distributor:	Warner Home Video (DVD)

53. *The Piano* (1993)
Writer:	Jane Campion
Director:	Jane Campion
Production Company	Australian Film Commission, CiBy, New South Wales Film and Television Office
Distributor:	Miramax Films

54. *The Graduate* (1967)
Writer:	Calder Willingham (Screenplay) &
Writer:	Buck Henry (Screenplay)
Writer:	Charles Webb (Novel)
Director:	Mike Nichols
Production Company:	Embassy Pictures
Production Company:	Lawrence Turman Inc.
Distributor:	MGM Home Entertainment (DVD)

55. *Requiem for A Dream* (2000)
Writer:	Hubert Selby Jr. (Screenplay) &
Writer:	Darren Aronofsky (Screenplay)
Writer:	Hubert Selby Jr. (Novel)
Director:	Darren Aronofsky
Production Company:	Artisan Entertainment
Production Company:	Bandeira Entertainment
Production Company:	Industry Entertainment
Production Company:	Protozoa Pictures
Production Company	Requiem for a Dream LLC
Production Company:	Sibling Productions
Production Company:	Thousand Words
Production Company:	Truth and Soul
Distributor:	Artisan Entertainment

56. *Citizen Kane* (1941)
Writer:	Herman J. Mankiewicz (Screenplay) &
Writer:	Orson Welles (Screenplay)
Writer:	John Houseman (Screenplay) (Uncredited)
Director:	Orson Welles
Production Company:	Mercury Productions
Production Company:	RKO Pictures
Distributor:	RKO Pictures Inc. (1941) USA Theatrical
Distributor:	Warner Home Video (DVD)

57. *Dances With Wolves* (1990)
Writer:	Michael Blake (Screenplay)
Writer:	Michael Blake (Novel)
Director:	Kevin Kostner
Production Company:	Tig Productions
Production Company:	Majestic Films International ns
Distributor:	Image Entertainment

SECTION **10** CAMERA POSITION

58. Film Element: Close-Up (CU)

A standard *close-up* includes the head and shoulders of the subject. An "extreme close-up" or ECU is a tighter shot filming only the eyes or lips, for example. A "close shot" may refer to a person or object, where a "close-up" usually refers to a person.

Film Example: *The Piano*

In Jane Campion's film *The Piano*, the protagonist is given a number of dramatic close-ups. In this first close-up, lasting about twenty seconds, Campion adds camera motion.

By staging it against dark, moving clouds, the close-up takes on a surreal quality. The camera circles around the character while keeping Ada's close-up intact. This creates an odd effect. It appears that Ada is stationary and the sky behind her is moving at a fixed speed. We expect characters to move, but backgrounds to remain stationary.

By subverting our expectations, Campion has created an ingenious effect. It is as though the strangely moving sky, filled with dark clouds, is a metaphor for the character's inner turmoil.

Now take a look at Image 4 taken from a different scene in the movie. Once again the intimate proximity the close-up delivers encourages our sympathy for the character. Notice how in both cases Campion augments the emotion of the shot by enlisting nature's help. Just as she used the stormy sky in the earlier example, she uses the streaming raindrops here to add meaning to the shot. The physical movement of these elements stands in direct contrast to Ada's frozen gaze. This juxtaposition further underscores how tightly Ada hides her emotions, even when no one is watching.

Dramatic Value

The closer we get to a character, the more sympathy we are likely to feel. This is because the close-up gives us a physical proximity usually reserved for those allowed within a character's intimate space. The longer we are held in close proximity, the more sympathy we feel. The close-up can also be used to evoke fear or revulsion when the audience is forced to be in close proximity to a character already established as a hated antagonist. In this case, the audience will want to escape from the forced proximity (see Film Element 62).

1.

2.

3.

4.

59. Film Element: Extreme Close-Up (ECU)

A *close-up* or *close shot* can be achieved in a variety of ways. It can be achieved by any lens, wide, normal, or telephoto. Each will bring different optical characteristics to the shot.

Dramatically, a close-up draws attention to an object by making the object larger-than-life. In the following example, Quentin Tarantino uses an ECU, or extreme close-up, to underscore pivotal dramatic elements.

Film Example: *Kill Bill: Vol. 1*

Black Mamba (Uma Thurman) has been in a coma after being shot in the head. In a bizarre twist of fate, a mosquito bite acts as catalyst for her recovery.

In depicting the life-changing "bite," Tarantino shoots both the scene's introductory bite and the flashback that follows as extreme close-ups.

Dramatic Value

An extreme close-up shows us objects and people differently than we see them. It calls attention to the subjects, making them more memorable visually. It also separates the scene from other scenes, underscoring the importance of the scene dramatically.

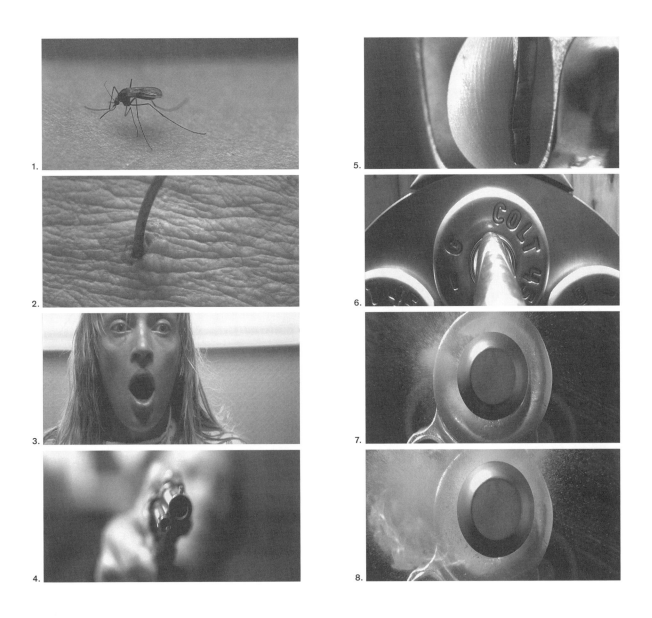

60. Film Element: Two-Shot

A *two-shot* is when two characters are filmed in a single shot. The characters are usually filmed from the mid-chest up. The two-shot can show harmony or disharmony depending on the scene. In these examples from *The Piano*, Campion is able to use contrasting two-shots to deepen our knowledge of character.

Film Example: *The Piano*

In *The Piano*, Ada (Holly Hunter) has arrived in New Zealand for an arranged marriage. Her young daughter accompanies her. The two have a symbiotic relationship. This is exaggerated as Hunter is mute and her daughter is accustomed to speaking for her.

Balanced Two-Shots

Campion exploits that aspect of the two-shot that can depict harmony. Whenever mother and daughter are in the same scene they most often appear in a balanced two-shot as they are in Images 1-3.

Imbalanced Two-Shots

When Campion shows Ada's marriage to her new husband she also uses a two-shot, the wedding photo seen in Image 4. Campion sabotages our expectations by using it to show the extent of the couple's disharmony. Ada looks away and her husband looks down as the rain pours down on the newlyweds. The image is imbalanced, and contrasts sharply with the harmonious shots of Ada and her daughter.

Dramatic Value

In having two people share one frame, the two-shot can suggest harmony or disharmony. By showing physical disharmony in the wedding photo, we immediately compare it to the conventional harmonious wedding shots we have seen. We also compare Ada's imbalanced wedding photo to the balanced shots with her daughter.

The comparisons are what enable the character reveals.

The Piano (1993) (Scene 28)

Screenplay: Jane Campion, 4th draft, 1991. Refers to image 1-2.

```
Sc 28    EXT    BAINES'    DAY
```

It is much later when BAINES emerges from his hut with a saddle over his arm. The two women are still there. ADA looks up at him expectantly.

FLORA mirrors her expression.

<pre>
                    BAINES
        I - can't - take - you there. I
        can't do it.
</pre>

He puts the saddle over a rail. He continues to saddle up, sneaking glances at them from under the horse and around its side. They watch him closely, not pleadingly, but stubbornly, eerily of one mind.

1.

2.

3.

4.

61. Film Element: Over-the-Shoulder Shot (OTS)

An *over-the-shoulder shot* (OTS) occurs when the camera is placed behind the shoulder of the character. The character's head and shoulders are seen in the foreground and are used as a framing device for the shot. Most often a second character is the subject of interest. In this way the two characters are "married" in the frame. Instead of separating the two characters in two separate close-ups or medium shots, the writer (and/or director) chooses to have both characters physically present in the shot. Depending on the content established in previous scenes, the over-the-shoulder shot can be used to suggest tension, intimacy, desire, hatred, imprisonment, or conspiracy, for example. It depends on the storyline and staging.

Film Example 1: *Chinatown*

This over-the-shoulder shot is the first time that Gittes (Jack Nicholson) and his love interest (Faye Dunaway) are in close physical proximity. They are brought together by a knife cut Nicholson has received caused by Nicholson's relentless determination to solve the case. The two are "married" together in the shot until Dunaway finishes attending Nicholson's wound. The tension builds as each tries to mask their attraction for each other.

Film Example 2: *The Piano*

Ada (Holly Hunter) is presented in a beautiful over-the-shoulder shot. The object of her attention is her piano that has been left behind on the beach. Although Ada and her piano share the same shot, what is exaggerated by this two-shot is the physical distance between them. This underscores Ada's longing for the piano and the difficulty she faces in regaining it.

Dramatic Value

The over-the-shoulder shot is like the two-shot in that two objects, usually characters, share the same space. The difference between this and the two-shot, is that one of the two characters faces us, the other doesn't. The physical connection can be used to convey information about the relationship. What is conveyed is dependent on staging and the storyline.

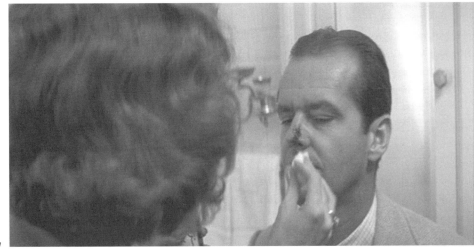

Chinatown

The Piano

62. Film Element: Point-of-View (POV)

A *point-of-view* shot (POV) is intended to represent the subjective view of a specific character. The camera lens is physically placed at the eye level of the character whose point-of-view we are seeing. In this way the audience sees what the character sees.

POV shots give audiences an exaggerated sense of intimacy with the character. This translates to sympathy if the POV belongs to the protagonist, and often fear, if it belongs to the antagonist.

In the example below, the POV shot is used to induce fear. The audience sees "Someone's POV" in a five-minute shot taken from the opening pages of *Halloween*. The shot ends with the stabbing death of a young woman.

Film Example: *Halloween*

The first character we meet in the script is simply introduced as "SOMEONE'S POV." We follow the POV for five minutes until "SOMEONE" stabs a young woman.

At the end of the sequence, the POV's identity is revealed to be Michael, a six-year-old boy.

We then flashforward fifteen years. We learn that a murderer is on the loose in the same town. As soon as we see the same extended POV shot, we immediately suspect that Michael has returned, now fifteen years older.

Dramatic Value

By coding the character with a unique camera shot, John Carpenter was able to flashforward fifteen years and immediately re-establish the character's identity without dialog or any other visual assistance.

The POV shot generally lends sympathy to the protagonist by allowing us to see through the character's eyes. Conversely, it can instill fear by forcing the same intimacy upon us with the antagonist.

Other Films

ET

Halloween (1978) (Scene 3)

Screenplay: John Carpenter and Debra Hill.

```
3  EXT./INT. MYERS HOUSE - NIGHT - SUBJECTIVE POV (PANAGLIDE)
```

It is night. We move toward the rear of the house through SOMEONE'S POV.
CAMERA MOVES UP to a Jack-O-Lantern glowing brightly on a windowsill. It
is a windy night and the curtains around the Jack-O-Lantern ruffle back
and forth. Suddenly we hear voices from inside the house.

>   SISTER (V.O.)
>   My parents won't be back till ten.
>
>   BOYFRIEND (V.O.)
>   Are you sure?

Then LAUGHTER.

The POV moves from the Jack-O-Lantern down to another window and
peers inside. We see the sister's bedroom through the blowing
curtains.

Into the bedroom comes the SISTER, 18, very pretty. She GIGGLES as
the BOYFRIEND jumps into the room. Alan, 18, he wears a Halloween
mask and a costume.

>   BOYFRIEND (V.O.; CONT'D)
>   We're all alone, aren't we?
>
>   SISTER (V.O.)
>   Michael's around someplace...

The boyfriend grabs the sister and kisses her.

>   SISTER (V.O.; CONT'D)
>   Take off that thing.

The boyfriend rips off his mask. He is a handsome young man
underneath. They kiss again, this time with more passion. The
boyfriend begins to unbutton the sister's blouse. She responds to him.

The POV swing away from the window and begins to restlessly pace back
and forth, agitated, disturbed. We HEAR THE SOUNDS of the sister and
boyfriend inside the bedroom growing more and more passionate.

Finally the POV moves back up to the window. Inside through the
moving curtains, we see the sister and the boyfriend on the bed,
naked, making love.

The POV springs back from the window and stalks quickly down the side
of the house, past the Jack-O-Lantern, around to a door. Quickly the
door is opened and the POV moves inside.

The POV glides silently through the house into the kitchen, up to a
drawer. The drawer is opened. A large BUTCHER KNIFE is withdrawn.

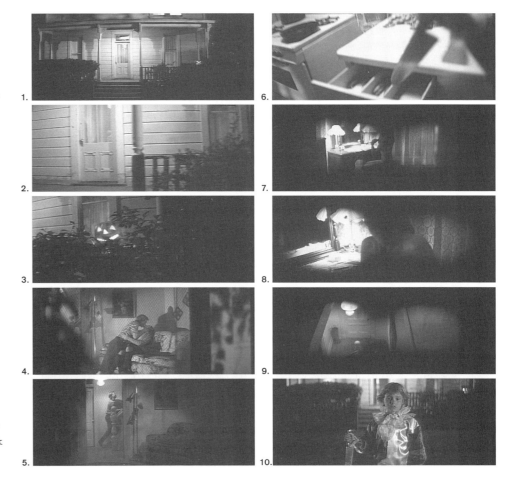

63. Film Element: Point-of-View (POV)

As mentioned in the previous example, a POV shot is usually reserved for the protagonist or antagonist in a film. As it significantly heightens sympathy or fear respectively, it is not randomly used.

In Steven Spielberg's *Jaws*, the shark's POV is used to instill our fear. Here are three examples of its use.

Film Example: *Jaws*

Act One
The first images we see appear simply as beautiful underwater shots of a young woman swimming. A moment later we see the young woman attacked and killed. Now we understand that the initial shots were actually a shark's POV.

Act Two
By scene 43, the audience has already seen a shark attack. When we now return to the same location and see vacationers swimming, our fear-antenna buzzes.

However, what sends our fear level off the charts is when Spielberg cuts below the surface to shoot the shark's POV (Image 2). Now we no longer see the floating vacationers as people, but as the shark sees them — *meals*. We notice how close they are, how unguarded, and how plentiful. By once again returning to an underwater POV shot, the audience is now trained to suspect the worst.

Act Three: Final Use
As soon as we see an underwater shot of the bottom of Richard Dreyfus' boat in Act Three, we know we are in for another attack (Image 3). We now assume the underwater shots represent the shark's POV. When Dreyfus dives down into the water, we know we are viewing him as the shark does: vulnerable, small, and unsure (Image 4). The repeated association of the POV shot with the shark immediately primes our fears.

Dramatic Value

Spielberg's POV shots not only showed us what the vacationers look like, but what we look like from beneath the water. It not only made us fear for the vacationers, but also ourselves. The POV shots made the audience do a paradigm shift, showing us the everyday from an entirely different point of view. In becoming the shark's signature shot, it also trained us to anticipate an attack.

Jaws (1975) (Scene 43)

Screenplay: Peter Benchley and Carl Gottlieb.
Final Draft. Novel: Peter Benchley.
Script excerpt refers to Image 2.

```
43. EXT. UNDERWATER - DAY
```

A fish-eye view of people lying on
rafts. From below we see the outlines
of swimmers, arms and legs dangling
tantalizingly in the blue water.
Traveling this way from raft to raft,
there comes a space of open water
followed by a quick view of a single
raft. A pair of feet kicking and arms
paddling produces bizarre underwater
vibrations, louder than human ears would
normally perceive.

1.

2.

3.

4.

64. Film Element: High-Angle

A *high-angle* shot occurs when the camera is placed above a subject with the lens pointing down. This makes the subject appear small and vulnerable.

Film Example 1: *Citizen Kane*

In *Citizen Kane*, Thompson, one of Ralston's journalists, visits Susan at a lounge where she sings. But the audience doesn't follow Thompson in through the front door. The camera crawls up over the roof and peaks down through the skylight minutes before Thompson arrives. This gives us an opportunity to catch an unguarded moment. From the vantage point of the high-angle we see a small seated figure, with her body bent over and her head resting on the table. The shot evokes our sympathy by making the figure look vulnerable and in despair.

The high-angle is then cut with an interior shot that continues the movement down from the roof until it settles on Susan seated at the table. Thompson now enters and sits with her. The two are composed in an over-the-shoulder shot that favors Susan. Susan now dominates the frame and her manner and dialog mirror the power the shot gives her (Images 7 and 8).

Dramatic Value

The contrast of the high-angle shot cut against the over-the-shoulder give us glimpses into both Susan's outer and inner personas. The high-angle is used for an unguarded moment showing her vulnerability; the over-the-shoulder shows her public persona, tough, shrill and embittered. What's interesting is how much sympathy the first high-angle lends to the second shot where Susan barks at the journalist. We now easily understand why.

Citizen Kane (1941)

Screenplay: Herman J. Mankiewicz and Orson Welles.

EXT. CHEAP CABARET--"EL RANCHO"--ATLANTIC CITY--NIGHT--1940

(Miniature--(Rain)

The first image to register is a sign:

"EL RANCHO"
FLOOR SHOW
SUSAN ALEXANDER KANE
TWICE MONTHLY

These words, spelled out in neon, glow out of the darkness at
the end of the fade out. Then there is lightning which reveals
a squalid roof-top on which the sign stands. Thunder again, and
faintly the sound of music from within. A light glows from a
skylight. The camera moves to this and closes in. Through the
splashes of rain, we see through the skylight down into the
interior of the cabaret. Directly below us at a table sits the
lone figure of a woman, drinking by herself.

1.

2.

3.

4.

5.

6.

7.

8.

65. Film Element: Low-Angle

A *low-angle* shot occurs when the camera is placed below the subject and the camera is pointing up. This causes the subject to appear larger-than-life. It transfers power to the subject, making it appear to dominate objects beneath it. Here are two examples from *ET*.

Film Example 1: *ET* (Redwoods)

When we first see ET walking along the forest, a high-angle is used. This makes ET appear small and vulnerable. The camera then cuts to a low-angle shot that appears to be ET's POV. Now we see ET looking up at the redwoods that surround him; this makes ET appear even more vulnerable as the low-angle shot exaggerates the relative size of the redwoods, making them appear to hover over the tiny figure.

Film Example 2: *ET* (Trucks)

In the next example, two pages later, we see ET's antagonists arrive. The low-angle is again used to suggest ET's POV. Shot from below, the trucks appear like huge growling monsters with blinding lights. We guess that ET is unclear on what the arriving trucks are: living species or robotic machines.

Dramatic Value

Low-angle shots make objects appear larger-than-life. In showing both the redwoods and trucks from this vantage point, power and mass is transferred to them. This contributes to our sense of ET's vulnerability. What adds further to our sympathy is that both shots are also designed as POV shots. In this way the audience gets to see the trucks and redwoods as ET sees them — huge and menacing.

Other Films

Citizen Kane

ET (1982) (Page 3, Scene 13)

Screenplay: Melissa Mathison, Rev. Sept. 8, 1981, Shooting Script.

```
13. HIGH ANGLE: THE CREATURE
```

THE CREATURE, still lit by his own conscience, turns and looks up at a towering fir tree. The RED LIGHT goes out. He walks into the forest.

```
EXT. FOREST - NIGHT
```

The SOUNDS of the forest rise: birds, babbling brooks, the twitter of insects. THE CREATURE moves deeper into the forest.

ET (1982) (Page 5, Scene 25)

Screenplay: Melissa Mathison, Rev. Sept. 8, 1981, Shooting Script.

```
37. THE CREATURE'S POV: THE CAR DOOR
```

The car door opens and a man steps out. Seen only from the waist down are: dark pants, heavy boots and a huge ring of KEYS hanging from his belt.

The KEYS make a tremendous racket, displacing all other sounds of the night.

66. Film Element: Hi-Lo Combined

As we said in the two previous sections:

a) A high-angle is placed above the subject pointing down. This makes the subject look small and vulnerable.

b) A low-angle is a shot taken from below, looking up at the subject. This makes an actor appear larger than in reality and appear to dominate the viewer.

Hitchcock exploited both characteristics in *Psycho* where he created a "hi-lo combination" and intercut between the two. Here's how it created suspense for the scene.

Film Example: *Psycho*

A young woman, Lila, a visitor to the Bates Motel, suspects that the owner, Mrs. Bates, might be alive in the house behind the hotel. Not knowing what she will find, or the reaction of Mrs. Bates' son, Norman, Lila climbs the steep steps up to the house.

High-Angle

Lila's climb is shot from above with a high-angle. It appears to be shot as the POV of someone inside the house. This makes Lila look physically small, vulnerable, and — possibly — *watched*.

Low-Angle

Then the film cuts to Lila's POV looking up at the house. The low-angle POV shot makes the house look huge and forbidding. It appears to hover over Lila. Then the camera cuts back to the house's POV, this time Lila is even closer — even more at risk.

Dramatic Value

By intercutting these two shots, Hitchcock has created a highly suspenseful scene. It's made even more frightening by implying that the high-angle might be the POV of an unseen character.

Psycho (1960)

Screenplay: Joseph Stephano. Revised Draft, Dec. 1, 1959.
Novel: Robert Bloch.

The scene is introduced with the note: "LILA: CAMERA ANGLES to include Lila and her point of view."

EXT. REAR OF MOTEL - S.C.U. LILA - (DAY)

Behind the hotel Lila hesitates. She looks ahead.

LONG SHOT - (DAY)

The old house standing against the sky.

CLOSE UP - (DAY)

Lila moves forward.

LONG SHOT - (DAY)

The CAMERA approaching the house.

CLOSE UP - (DAY)

Lila glances toward the back of Norman's parlor. She moves on.

LONG SHOT - (DAY)

The house coming nearer.

CLOSE-UP - (DAY)

Lila looks up at the house. She moves forward purposefully.

S.L.S. - (DAY)

The house and the porch.

CLOSE UP - (DAY)

Lila stops at the house and looks up. She glances back.
She turns to the house again.

S.L.S. - (DAY)

The CAMERA MOUNTS the steps to the porch.

C.U. - (DAY)

Lila puts out her hand.

S.C.U. - (DAY)

Lila pushes the door open. We see the hallway.
Lila ENTERS PAST CAMERA.

1.

2.

3.

Chapter Credits By Film Element

58. *Kill Bill: Vol. 1* (2003)

Writer:	Quentin Tarantino (Screenplay)
Writer:	QI and U1 (Character of the Bride)
Director:	Quentin Tarantino
Production Company:	Miramax Films
Production Company:	A Band Apart
Production Company:	Super Cool ManChu
Distributor:	Miramax Films

59. *The Piano* (1993)

Writer:	Jane Campion
Director:	Jane Campion
Production Company	Australian Film Commission, CiBy, New South Wales Film and Television Office
Distributor:	Miramax Films

60. *The Piano* (1993)
Same as above.

61. *Chinatown* (1974)

Writer:	Robert Towne
Writer:	Roman Polanski (Uncredited)
Director:	Roman Polanski
Production Company:	Paramount Pictures
Production Company:	Long Road
Production Company:	Penthouse
Distributor:	Paramount Home Video (USA) (DVD)

62. *Halloween* (1978)

Writer:	John Carpenter (Screenplay) &
Writer:	Debra Hill (Screenplay)
Director:	John Carpenter
Production Company:	Compass International
Production Company:	Falcon Films
Distributor:	Anchor Bay Entertainment

63. *Jaws* (1975)

Writer:	Peter Benchley (Screenplay)
Writer:	Carl Gottlieb (Screenplay)
Writer:	Peter Benchley (Novel)
Director:	Steven Spielberg
Production Company:	Universal Pictures
Production Company:	Zanuck/Brown Productions
Distributor:	Universal Studios Home Video (USA) (DVD)

64. *Citizen Kane* (1941)

Writer:	Herman J. Mankiewicz (Screenplay) &
Writer:	Orson Welles (Screenplay)
Writer:	John Houseman (Screenplay) (Uncredited)
Director:	Orson Welles
Production Company:	Mercury Productions
Production Company:	RKO Pictures
Distributor:	RKO Pictures Inc. (1941) USA Theatrical
Distributor:	Warner Home Video (DVD)

65. *ET* (1982)

Writer:	Melissa Mathison (Screenplay)
Director:	Steven Spielberg
Production Company:	Amblin Entertainment
Production Company:	Universal Pictures
Distributor:	Columbia TriStar Home Video (USA) (DVD)

66. *Psycho* (1960)

Writer:	Joseph Stephano
Writer:	Robert Bloch (Novel)
Director:	Alfred Hitchcock
Production Company:	Shamley Productions
Distributor:	Paramount Pictures
Distributor:	Universal Home Entertainment (USA) (DVD)

SECTION **11**   CAMERA

MOTION

67. Film Element: Static Shot

A *static shot* occurs when the camera is locked down on a tripod. Though the objects within the frame might move, the view of the scene is fixed like that seen through a window or framed by a proscenium arch.

Film Example: *Klute*

First Static Wide-Shot

The opening shot of Alan J. Pakula's *Klute* is a static wide-angle shot that looks like a picture postcard of an American family sharing a holiday dinner. The shot is still, perfectly balanced. Notice the symmetry of the dining room table and chairs, the window panes and the two balanced flower pots in the center pane. Each pot is hung along the same plane and is the same size.

After a moment the camera pans around the table introducing us to individual guests. The scene concludes with two static shots of the husband and wife toasting each other. Then we cut to the husband's chair in another static shot.

The husband's chair is now empty.

Second Static Wide-Shot

Now we return to the same wide shot that opened the film — the static proscenium arch shot of the dining room table. Now we realize this is another time. The frame is darkly lit and the children and family members are gone. The symmetry is also lost. One character stands with his back to us. One sits at an angle to the camera. There is a huge empty space behind the wife not present in the opening shot. Against the window panes, the flower pots hang asymmetrically.

Dramatic Value

A static shot is easily compared to another similarly composed static shot. Their stillness helps us see changes. In this pairing, the symmetry of the first shot helps us notice deviations of the second shot. We know by comparing the two static shots that something terrible has happened.

Script Note

You will notice that the cutting in the movie is slightly different than what is suggested in the script excerpt that follows.

Klute (1971)

Screenplay: Andy and Dave Lewis, June 26, 1970, Final.

```
1. INT. DINING ROOM - TOM GRUNEMANN HOUSE - DAY
```

CLOSE SHOT of TOM GRUNEMANN, attractive young executive,
sitting at the head of the dining room table carving a
turkey for Thanksgiving Day dinner. There are joyous sounds
of celebration. The CAMERA PANS around the table revealing
the happy family and guests. Among them are KLUTE and CABLE.

Camera stops at Mrs. Grunemann who sits at the foot of the
table opposite her husband. She smiles across at him with
pleasure. We cut to Tom Grunemann smiling back at her. We
cut back to a close-up of Mrs. Grunemann looking back at her
husband with love.

We cut back to Tom Grunemann's chair - only now it is empty.
The joyous sounds disappear on this cut. It appears that Tom
Grunemann has disappeared before our eyes. One moment he is
there, and the next moment he is gone. The camera pans back
down the table, and now it is empty except for Grunemann's
children and Mrs. Grunemann. She is now dressed in something
dark. She and the three children sit eating another meal in
emptiness. She has changed from a joyous woman to a woman
bereaved.

1.

2.

3.

4.

68. Film Element: Pan

A pan usually occurs when the camera is seated on a tripod and pivots to the left or the right along a horizontal plane. It can also be handheld. In the process of moving the camera, new information is revealed. It could be about the parameters of a location, an important clue, or a hidden character.

Film Example: *Dances with Wolves*

In the opening scene in *Dances with Wolves* a pan reveals John J. Dunbar's point-of-view as he scans the bloody surgery tools nearby. In having seen what Dunbar sees, when Dunbar decides against the amputation, we understand the decision.

Dramatic Value

Instead of cutting to reveal information, panning offers another option. This includes depicting the information in real time with continuous movement. The movement suggests a certain fluidity. A POV shot is one kind of pan; there are many others.

1.

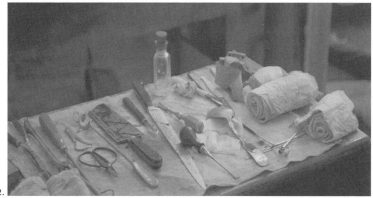

2.

3.

69. Film Element: Tilt-Up (Character)

A *tilt-up* is when the camera moves up on a vertical axis. It is usually used as a reveal.

Film Example: *The Professional*

The tilt-up is used to introduce the character of young Mathilda in *The Professional*. The slow continuous tilt-up asks the audience to notice the contradictions in her clothing. She is at the same time child and woman; tough and gentle. The tilt-up starts with her boots, moves over her comic book leotards, past her teenager's jewelry to her gentle, vulnerable face that is hidden behind an ornate railing. The tilt-up gives the audience the time to take in each wardrobe element separately and notice their contradiction, which is central to her character.

Dramatic Value

A close-range tilt is like a moving close-up. It directs the audience to details that they may not otherwise notice.

Other Films

Citizen Kane (See Film Element 23)

The Professional (Léon) (1994) (Scene 7, Page 6)

Screenplay: Luc Besson, Seaside, 1993.

Though the tilt is not referenced here, the contradictions that the tilt will later capture are established. Here's the excerpt from the script.

```
38.INT. APARTMENT BUILDING - DAY
LEON walks up the stairs. He seems a little tired.

Arriving on his floor, LEON comes across a 12-year GIRL sitting
on the stairs. She hides her cigarette when she sees him.

The GIRL is adorable - half-angel, half-devil. She's not yet
a woman, but she's also no longer a child. In any case, she's
extremely attractive.

They exchange distant smiles. LEON notices her black-eye and
bruised cheek.

He walks past her, then walks back.
```

1.

2.

3.

70. Film Element: Tilt-Down

A *tilt-down* is when the camera moves down on a vertical axis. It is usually used as a reveal.

Film Example 1: *Fargo*

The first example from *Fargo* is a conventional use of the tilt-down. The top of the shot catches a freeway sign. The bottom of the tilt picks up a car. The tilt connects the two, establishing the car's location.

Film Example 2: *Fargo*

The second example is almost identical. Instead of a freeway sign announcing location, the scene picks out a huge, eerie statue of Paul Bunyan. The statue has a plaque announcing the town ahead, in this case Brainerd. Shot at night and starting with a slim slice of Bunyan's forehead, the shot gives the audience location information as well as setting up atmosphere.

Dramatic Value

Both shots set up location. One links a specific car with the location, the other focuses on atmosphere. The Paul Bunyan shot also underscores the forbidding size of Bunyan — it's as though only a moving shot could capture all of him. This is similar to the tilt-up used to capture Kane's immense estate mentioned earlier (Film Element 23).

Script Note

The script excerpt refers to Film Example 1, a staple use of the concept. It shows writers how to express the idea. The images of Paul Bunyan, Film Example 2, were included to show a more dramatic use of the camera move.

Fargo (1996) (Page 61)

Screenplay: Joel Coen & Ethan Coen, Draft: Nov. 2, 1994.

Film Example 1

```
A GREEN FREEWAY SIGN

Pointing to the exit for the MINNEAPOLIS INTERNATIONAL
AIRPORT.

A tilt down reveals Carl behind the wheel of the Ciera
taking the turn.

An airport sign reads LONG TERM PARKING.

Carl takes a ticket and drives up the parking ramp.
```

Film Example 2

1.

2.

3.

71. Film Element: Rotation

Because of the stability normally desired, a camera rotation is usually created by rotating the camera when secured on a tripod. A camera rotation spins the image around causing a disorienting effect. Here's how a 90-degree rotation was used in *Bound*.

Film Example: *Bound*

Ceasar, a mobster, arrives home with a sack full of bloodied cash. The next day his girlfriend tells her friend, Corky, about the events of the evening. We cut back and forth between the storyteller in the present, and the events of the night before.

As the events occur over an extended period, a camera rotation is slipped in the middle of the storytelling. It divides the story into two units acting like a curtain drop in theatre or the chaptering of a novel.

In this instance the "two chapters" represent a change in the evening's tone: from "mobster-normalcy" to "mobster-surreal." The rotation indicates the changeover.

Dramatic Value

The movement of the camera itself works as a metaphor characterizing the tone of the evening. In this case the camera rotation works to separate two parts of a recollection.

Script Note

Notice in the script excerpt that writers-directors Larry Wachowski and Andy Wachowski don't describe the camera move, they just describe its effect.

Script Excerpt: We cut in at the end of the scene where Ceasar's girlfriend, Violet, begins to explain the events from the night before. Here's how we come into the camera rotation.

Other Films

Apocalypse Now (opening dissolves)

See images from *Apocalpyse Now* on the next page.

Bound (1996) Page 43)

Screenplay: Larry Wachowski & Andy Wachowski, First Draft, September 28, 1994.

```
INT. CORKY'S APARTMENT - DAY

                   VIOLET
          It was unreal...

Moving in on her face.

MATCH CUT TO:

Benjamin Franklin's face on a hundred
dollar bill.

INT. CEASAR'S APARTMENT

Franklin's face rotates as we pull back
seeing rows of bills carefully paper-
clipped to lines of string.

                   VIOLET (V.O.)
          Hundred's, paper clipped
          everywhere like leaves.

Eyes filled with green, Violet turns
inside the laundry lines of money until
she sees Ceasar.

Wearing his undershirt, he is across
the room standing at the ironing board,
ironing every single bill.

He seems to have one eye on her, one eye
on his work.

                   VIOLET (V.O.)
          Then one by one he ironed all
          of it.

He sprays starch across several bills and
presses the steaming iron to them.

                   CORKY (V.O.)
          Did he sleep?
```

Bound

1.

2.

3.

4.

Apocalypse Now

1.

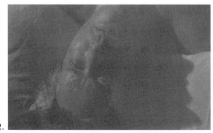

2.

3.

4.

72. Film Element: Tracking Shot

Technically, a *tracking shot* occurs when the camera is mounted on a dolly and glides along tracks. This allows the camera to move smoothly along a fixed path. Much like train tracks, the camera tracks can form a linear or curved pattern. Today, the term tracking shot is also used to refer to shots that effect the look of a tracking shot. The camera may be mounted on a car, dolly, or other moving vehicle that "tracks" with the subject.

Tracking is used for a variety of situations. The camera can track along the faces of a jury as it does in the opening courtroom scene in *American Beauty*. This way the audience can study each individual face as they are revealed in the "moving close-up." The camera can also track around an object, as it does the jewel thieves in the opening diner scene in *Reservoir Dogs*.

In *Marathon Man* and *The 400 Blows*, extended tracking shots occur as the camera runs alongside its protagonist.

One of the most ingenious uses of a tracking shot is seen in *Fatal Attraction*. Here's the set-up. It's an incredible shot.

Film Example: *Fatal Attraction*

Dan (Michael Douglas) has a perfect life. Then one day he decides to go for drinks with an attractive colleague (Glen Close). While the two talk, a tracking shot is brilliantly used to show us the two faces of Michael's character.

The shot that precedes the tracking shot is an over-the-shoulder shot favoring Douglas (Image 1). This is Douglas' "good side" where he talks about:

a) how as a dutiful son and lawyer he helped his mother with her divorce. Then we cut behind Douglas, and starting on his "good side," track over to his "bad side" (Image 2-4).

b) Now the conversation shifts as Douglas and Close discuss "discretion" which leads to their weekend fling. In one brilliant tracking shot we go from Douglas' "good side" to his "bad side" and from dutiful son to cheating husband.

Dramatic Value

The camera movement parallels Michael's outer and inner self. It's a brilliant, unexpected use of the device.

Other Films

Marathon Man

American Beauty

The 400 Blows

1.

2.

3.

4.

5.

6.

73. Film Element: Circular

Circular motion is an effect that can be created with a hand-held camera, Steadicam, or tracks.

A circular shape can be linked to any number of ideas. In the opening scenes of the following two films, circular motion is exploited to plant the idea of conspiracy. Circular motion is also used to establish the idea of groups — insiders and outsiders — upon which both stories depend.

Film Example: *Reservoir Dogs*

Reservoir Dogs uses a circular tracking shot to introduce its "den of thieves" — eight jewelry thieves seated in a circle at a Denny's-like diner. At first the camera circles around their table. The audience is given the role of "outsider." By the end of the scene, our degree of access changes. The camera is now stationary, seated on a tripod, and positioned between characters at the table. It's as though the jewel thieves have pushed a chair up to the table and invited the audience to join in. Now we see unobstructed close-ups, and longer takes with extended dialog passages. The chair is pushed back from the others just a little, indicating privileged access, but not full membership.

The circular indicates outsider status, and the contrasting stationary camera indicates "insider" status. Later we will learn that we have been watching is the aftermath of the thieves conspire to pull off a robbery and against each other. Despite the appearance of access, and what appears to "insider" status, we have no real knowledge yet of what the scene means. This is almost identical to the set-up in *The Conversation*.

Film Example: *The Conversation* (Not Pictured)

As in *Reservoir Dogs*, *The Conversation* uses the circle to introduce the idea of conspiracy. In the opening scene, the camera follows the movie's yet unidentified conspirators who move in a circle around a noon-day crowd. Later we will understand that they are conspirators, not victims.

Dramatic Value

In both cases the circular is used to foreshadow a conspiracy that is later revealed. Having the camera's motion physically externalize thematic ideas greatly deepens the audience engagement and overall power of the storytelling.

1.

2.

3.

4.

74. Film Element: Push-in — Pull-Out

A *Push-In* occurs when the camera is seated on a dolly and "pushes in" toward an object. This causes the view to narrow. A Push-In and Track-In are often used interchangeably. Traditionally, however, a Track-In means that the dolly is mounted on tracks.

A *Pull-Out* occurs when the camera is seated on a dolly and pulls away from an object. This causes the view to widen. Pull-Out, Push-Out, Pull-Back, or Widen-Out are often used interchangeably.

Camera Move: A Push-In on one object in one location, followed by a Pull-Out on an identical or similar object in another location is a staple technique. Often it is just done as an effect, to get in and out of locations. But it can also be used with dramatic purpose — one of which is comparison. The audience sees the same object in two environments and immediately compares them. Here's how a "Push-In — Pull-Out" was used in Fargo.

Film Example: *Fargo*

Two thugs are holed up in a cabin on the outskirts of town. Their kidnap victim is seated in a chair with her hands tied and a toque pulled down over her face. One of the thugs looks around him. He stares at the rhythmic breathing of his victim's breath as it streams through the toque. He looks over at his partner who is pounding at the broken TV. As the thug focuses on his partner's idiotic behavior, the camera pushes in until only the TV screen is seen. We hold on the screen until a clear picture forms. Then the camera pulls back. As it pulls back we realize it's a different TV in a different location. We then cut to the new TV viewer who is Marge. She is in bed with her sleepy husband beside her.

Dramatic Value

Both scenes have couples watching TV late at night. One is a pair of reckless thugs, the other a blissful couple expecting a baby. The combined shot helps to remind us of the different paths life can take. The shot uses a singular object to contrast two environments and their characters.

Fargo (1996)

Screenplay: Joel Coen & Ethan Coen, Draft: Nov. 2, 1994.

We are jumping in mid-scene...

INT. CABIN

WE TRACK IN ON CARL SHOWALTER, WHO STANDS OVER AN OLD black-and-white television. It plays nothing but snow. Carl is banging on it as he mutters:

> CARL
> ... days…be here for days with a -
> Dammit! - a goddamn mute … NOTHIN' TO DO … AND THE
> FUCKING - DAMMIT!....

Each "dammit" brings a pound of his fist on the TV.

> CARL
> ... TV doesn't even... plug me in, MAN...
> GIMME A - DAMMIT! - signal... Plug me into the
> ozone, baby... Plug me into the ozone - FUCK!...

WITH ONE LAST BANG WE CUT:

BACK TO THE TELEVISION SET

In extreme close-up an insect is lugging a worm.

> TV VOICE-OVER
> The bark beetle carries the worm to the nest...
> where it will feed its young for up to six weeks....

A pull back from the screen reveals that we are in Marge's house.

Marge and Norm are watching television in bed. From the TV we hear insects chirring.

1.

2.

3.

4.

75. Film Element: Crane

A *crane shot* is created by attaching the camera to the arm of a crane. The camera can be raised or lowered. The crane can also be stationary or moving. A crane is often used to deliver high-angle shots that look down on a scene.

Film Example: *Touch of Evil*

In a still unparalleled scene, Orson Welles opens *Touch of Evil* with a legendary crane shot. The shot starts with a close-up of a ticking clock, then pulls up and over a busy border town at night. The shot moves smoothly along linear planes, its movement seemingly prompted by anticipating the action.

Dramatic Value

The opening of *Touch of Evil* has an almost omniscient quality. This has to do with its seemingly effortless ability to reveal "secrets" and pertinent events almost suggesting foreknowledge. The overall effect is a highly controlled, smoothly rendered picture of the events.

Other Films

The Player (homage to this shot from *Touch of Evil*)

1.

2.

3.

76. Film Element: Handheld

A handheld shot occurs when the camera is removed from the tripod and is literally "handheld" by the camera operator. The effect creates an unstable image. The bumpier the shot, the more instability can be suggested. The impact of the shot is often exaggerated by juxtaposing it with a smooth shot or one that is locked down.

Film Example: *Touch of Evil*

In the filmed version of *Touch of Evil* the legendary crane shot starts with a close-up, then moves to a high-angle. It then continually reconfigures itself moving across town while we wait for the ticking bomb to go off.

First Shot — Order
The opening crane shot is orchestrated with precision and parallels the ordered world of a young couple when suddenly—a car bomb goes off.

Second Shot — Chaos
Once the bomb explodes the camera changes. The smooth movement of the crane shot is replaced by the chaotic movement of the incoming shot.

Script Note

In the script version Orson Welles uses a handheld shot to suggest the instability in the aftermath scene. He has a camera operator run behind the lead characters through the crowd.

In the filmed version the chaos is expressed by placing the camera on a bumpy vehicle that rides in front of the characters shooting back at them. The bumpy ride helped further realize the chaos a handheld shot suggests.

Dramatic Value

A handheld shot is often used to suggest instability. It is especially effective when contrasted to a stable image.

Touch of Evil (1958)

Screenplay: Orson Welles, Rev. Final Screenplay, Feb. 5, 1957.

We jump in at the end of the crane shot scene. The camera then changes to handheld. See Reverse Angle below.

```
Border Check Point

---

Just as their lips meet -- there is a deafening
explosion! A sudden glare of flame lights the darkness
ahead…

QUICK FLASH - THE FLAMING WRECK OF THE CAR

A great hub-bub as a crowd starts to gather. Distantly
the shrilling of police WHISTLES is heard... and then
the screams of an approaching SIREN…

REVERSE ANGLE

The following sequence photographed with a hand camera-
the operator following Mike and Susan through the crowd
on foot.

Mike, followed by Susan, is running forward when an OLD
MAN (a field-hand type) dashes by, going in the other
direction. Mike stops him and there is a swift exchange
in Spanish.

                    SUSAN
          Mike! --what's happened?

The old man dashes OFF SCENE.

Mike continues hurrying toward the scene of the
accident, Susan tagging along at his side.

                    MIKE
          It exploded --

                    SUSAN
          (breathlessly, by now
          they are almost running)

     Just the car? --How could it do that?
```

The scene continues---

77. Film Element: Handheld

Film Example: *Pulp Fiction*

As discussed in the previous section, the handheld shot can be used to suggest instability, especially when contrasted with a stable, locked-down shot. In this well-known scene from *Pulp Fiction,* chaos erupts when a drug dealer, his girlfriend, and clients realize that the woman on their carpet is about to overdose.

Here the camera zips back and forth between screaming characters. It's as though the handheld camera is depicting the POV of the audience, and the audience itself is standing in the middle of the room.

Dramatic Value

As both examples illustrate, the handheld shot is made more effective when it is contrasted with its opposite, a locked-down shot. It can add further dimension when used as a POV shot as well.

Pulp Fiction (1994)

Screenplay: Quentin Tarantino, May 1993.

Stories by: Quentin Tarantino & Roger Roberts Avary

WE START in Lance's and Jody's bedroom.

Jody, in bed, throws off the covers and stands up. She's wearing a long tee-shirt with a picture of Fred Flintstone on it.

We follow HANDHELD behind her as she opens the door, walking through the hall into the living room.

                    JODY
          It's only one-thirty in the goddamn
          mornin'! What the fuck's goin' on
          out here?

As she walks in the living room, she sees Vincent and Lance standing over Mia, who's lying on the floor in the middle of the room.

From here on in, everything in this scene is frantic, like a DOCUMENTARY in an emergency ward, with the big difference here being nobody knows what the fuck they're doing.

                    JODY
          Who's she?

Lance looks up at Jody.

                    LANCE
          Get that black box in the bedroom I
          have with the adrenalin shot.

1.

2.

3.

78. Film Element: Steadicam

The Steadicam was introduced in the 1970s and immediately appeared in films like *Rocky* and *The Shining*. Since then it has been a staple tool used in motion pictures.

The Steadicam takes the camera off the fixed tripod and gives it the freedom of a handheld shot. However, the Steadicam's stabilization device smoothes out the bumpiness of the handheld shot making Steadicam shots appear to "float."

Here's how Martin Scorsese used an extended Steadicam shot to deepen characterization in *Goodfellas*.

Film Example: *Goodfellas*

Henry is an up-and-coming mobster. In this scene he has decided to introduce his girlfriend, who is an outsider, to his mob life. Rather than take her through the front door of the Copacabana and wait in line, he takes her through the back way. The Steadicam floats with the couple through long basement hallways and the huge kitchen. Throughout, Henry tips busboys, chefs, waiters, and the maitre d', impressing his new girlfriend. Henry's exposure of his hidden mob life to his girlfriend is paralleled by the backdoor view we are given of the club.

Dramatic Value

In this scene the Steadicam's fluidity has been exploited to suggest Henry's ease of access to the spoils of the good life and his dream-like good luck.

The Steadicam's ability to move in and out of places, then suddenly spin around to a wide shot has also been exploited in horror films like *The Shining* and the *Halloween* series. On the other hand its fluid quality has also been used to suggest dreams and fantasies.

Other Films

Rocky (Philadelphia courthouse stairs)

Halloween (see introductory POV shot)

Bonfire of the Vanities

The Shining

Goodfellas (1990) (Scene 46, Page 35)

Screenplay: Nicolas Pileggi. Script Draft 1/12/89.
Book: *Wiseguy*, by Nicholas Pileggi. See Chapter Credits
for final writing credits.

EXT. COPACABANA - NIGHT

HENRY gives the keys and a rolled-up twenty-dollar
bill to the DOORMAN at the building across the
street and steers KAREN toward the Copa.

          KAREN
     What are you doing? What about
     the car?

          HENRY
        (while pushing her
        through the crowd
        waiting to get in)

     He watches it for me. It's
     better than waiting at a garage.

WE SEE HENRY deftly steer KAREN away from the
Copa's main entrance and down the basement steps. A
HUGE BODYGUARD, eating a sandwich in the stairwell,
gives HENRY a big "hello." WE SEE HENRY walk right
through the basement kitchen, which is filled with
CHINESE and LATINO COOKS and DISHWASHERS who pay
no attention. KAREN is being dragged along, open-
mouthed, at the scene. HENRY starts up a stained
kitchen staircase through a pair of swinging doors
and suddenly KAREN sees she is inside the main
room. The harried MAITRE D' (he is surrounded by
customers clamoring for their tables) waves happily
at HENRY and signals to a CAPTAIN. WE SEE a table
held aloft by TWO WAITERS wedging their way toward
the stage and plant the table smack in front of
what had until that moment been a ringside table.
As HENRY leads KAREN to their seat, she sees that
he is nodding and shaking hands with MANY of the
OTHER GUESTS. WE SEE HENRY quietly slip twenty-
dollar-bills to the WAITERS.

1.

2.

3.

4.

5.

6.

7.

8.

79. Film Element: Aerial

An *aerial shot* is taken from an elevated site, such as a plane, helicopter, or mountain top. In delivering the image from a bird's eye point-of-view, the shot's graphics more easily lend themselves to symbolic use. Here's how Jane Campion put an aerial shot to work in *The Piano*.

Film Example: *The Piano*

After a day at the beach, Ada (Holly Hunter) heads toward home. Hunter's young daughter trails her like a duck. Their footsteps leave a long sweeping trail in the mud. From some distance, Hunter's soon-to-be-lover (Harvey Keitel) looks after the two trying to decide if he should follow the path laid down by Hunter.

The aerial shot enables us to graphically see Keitel make his decision. From the aerial shot we can see the long path cut in the mud with Keitel positioned on one side, Hunter and her daughter on the other. When Keitel traces Hunter footsteps along the path, we know he has made a decision to pursue Hunter romantically.

The shot is also able to reveal the "beach art" left behind from their day at the beach. It's not clear what it is. It could be a be a seahorse, maybe a treble clef. In either case, it dramatically presents Ada's yet unseen whimsical nature.

Dramatic Value

The aerial shot is able to graphically depict Keitel's decision to pursue Hunter. It also shows us the stunning image of the "beach art" which could only be fully seen from this height.

Other Films

Psycho

American Beauty

The Piano (1993) (Scene 31)

Screenplay: Jane Campion, 4th draft, 1991.

```
Sc 31 EXT. BEACH - NIGHT
```

```
From a helicopter, the camera tracks along the
beach, following the crashing wave line, to find
the piano.
```

*Script Note: In the film the aerial tracking shot
"finds" the seahorse-treble clef, instead of the
piano.*

1.

2.

Chapter Credits By Film Element

67. Klute (1971)

Writer:	Andy Lewis (Screenplay)
Writer	David Lewis (Screenplay)
Director:	Alan J. Pakula
Production Company:	Gus Productions
Production Company:	Warner Bros.
Distributor:	Warner Bros.

68. Dances With Wolves (1990)

Writer:	Michael Blake (Screenplay)
Writer:	Michael Blake (Novel)
Director:	Kevin Kostner
Production Company:	Tig Productions
Production Company:	Majestic Films International
Distributor:	Image Entertainment

69. The Professional (1994)

Writer:	Luc Besson (Screenplay)
Director:	Luc Besson
Production Company:	Gaumont International
Production Company:	Les Films du Dauphin
Distributor:	Columbia TriStar Home Video (USA) DVD

70. Fargo (1996)

Writer:	Joel Coen (Screenplay) &
Writer:	Ethan Coen (Screenplay)
Director:	Joel Coen
Director:	Ethan Coen (Uncredited)
Production Company:	Gramercy Pictures
Production Company:	Polygram Filmed Entertainment
Production Company:	Working Title Films
Distributor:	Concorde Home Entertainment (1998) DVD
Distributor:	Gramercy (USA) Theatrical

71. Bound (1996)

Writer:	The Wachowski Brothers & The Wachowski Brothers
Director:	The Wachowski Brothers & The Wachowski Brothers

Production Company:	Dino de Laurentiis Productions
Production Company:	Spelling Films
Distributor:	Gramercy Pictures

72. Fatal Attraction (1987)

Writer:	James Dearden (Screenplay) (also earlier version)
Writer:	Nicholas Meyer
Director:	Adrian Lyne
Production Company:	Paramount Pictures
Distributor:	Paramount Home Video (USA) (DVD)

73. Reservoir Dogs (1992)

Writer:	Quentin Tarantino (Screenplay)
Writer:	Roger Avary (Background radio dialog writer)
Director:	Quentin Tarantino
Production Company:	Live Entertainment
Production Company:	Dog Eat Dog Productions
Distributor:	Artisan Entertainment 2002 (USA) (DVD)
Distributor:	Miramax Films

74. Fargo (1996)

Writer:	Joel Coen (Screenplay) &
Writer:	Ethan Coen (Screenplay)
Director:	Joel Coen
Director:	Ethan Coen (Uncredited)
Production Company:	Gramercy Pictures
Production Company:	Polygram Filmed Entertainment
Production Company:	Working Title Films
Distributor:	Concorde Home Entertainment (1998) (DVD)
Distributor:	Gramercy (USA) Theatrical

75. Touch of Evil (1958)

Writer:	Orson Welles (Screenplay)
Writer:	Paul Monash (Screenplay Uncredited)

Writer:	Whit Masterson (Novel: *Badge of Evil*)
Director:	Orson Welles
Production Company:	Universal International Pictures
Production Company:	Universal Pictures
Distributor:	MCA/Universal Pictures

76. Touch of Evil (1958)

Same as above.

77. Pulp Fiction (1994)

Writer:	Quentin Tarantino (Screenplay)
Writer:	Quentin Tarantino (Stories)
Writer:	Robert Avary (Stories)
Director:	Quentin Tarantino
Production Company:	A Band Apart
Production Company:	Jersey Films
Production Company:	Miramax Films
Distributor:	Miramax Home Entertainment (USA) (DVD

78. Goodfellas (1990)

Writer:	Nicholas Pileggi (Screenplay &
Writer:	Martin Scorsese (Screenplay
Writer:	Nicholas Pileggi (Book: *Wis Guy*)
Director:	Martin Scorsese
Production Company:	Warner Brothers
Distributor:	Warner Brothers Home Vid

79. The Piano (1993)

Writer:	Jane Campion
Director:	Jane Campion
Production Company	Australian Film Commissio CiBy, New South Wales Filr and Television Office
Distributor:	Miramax Films

LIGHTING

80. Film Element: Rembrandt Lighting (Light versus Dark)

Rembrandt lighting is lighting that intentionally creates contrasts of light and dark. High contrast lighting or *chiaroscuro* was developed by the Italian painter Caravaggio. The lighting often appears to come from spotlights shining on the action while other areas disappear into unlit shadows. The technique is said to achieve a heightened dramatization or greater truth-to-life. It is often reserved for pivotal scenes expressing key philosophical questions of good and evil, life and death. Here's how it was used in *Apocalypse Now*.

Film Example: *Apocalypse Now*

In *Apocalypse Now*, Captain Willard's (Martin Sheen) assignment is to locate Colonel Kurtz and terminate. However, we know from the opening scenes that Willard is on the brink of madness himself. When Willard finally locates Kurtz (Marlon Brando), the question is whether Willard will be able to hold onto his own sanity and "terminate," or be felled by madness himself.

Here are three examples of how Rembrandt lighting contributed to the scene.

Shot 1
As the scene opens Willard kneels before a backlit curtain waiting for an interview with Kurtz. Because the curtain is lit, and Willard is seen in silhouette, Kurtz's unseen presence dominates. The backlit curtain also gives Kurtz a mystical quality.

Shot 2
We then cut to Kurtz behind the curtain. Kurtz rises from his rest, his massive head emerging from darkness. The rest of the frame is black, making his head appear detached from his body, suggesting madness. As Kurtz straightens his head, only the rim of his skull is lit. It appears like the sliver of the moon or "lune," subtly suggesting lunacy.

Shot 3
In the last shot taken from this scene Kurtz rinses his head while Willard explains that Kurtz's superiors believe he is mad. Now Kurtz's head is fully spotlighted, the water runs like gold. Despite our associations with water and cleansing, Kurtz cannot rid himself of his demons. It's an incredible image, timeless and disturbing.

Dramatic Value
Chiaroscuro dramatizes Kurtz's insanity with its high-contrast lighting The backlighting, often associated with moral goodness, is subverted to suggest madness.

81. Film Element: TV Lighting

TV lighting, especially sitcom lighting, is conventionally bright, flat, and shadowless.

Film Example: *Natural Born Killers*

In *Natural Born Killers,* Mallory, the female protagonist, answers her boyfriend's question about her parents with a flashback. The flashback is in the form of what momentarily appears to be a conventional sitcom. The lighting is flat, the shots are TV-styled, and a sitcom laugh track follows each punchline.

The content, however, is anything but sitcom fare. The sitcom's plot deals with Mallory's sexual abuse at the hands of her father, and the overall physical and psychological brutality of his family.

Dramatic Value

The scene takes a known medium and stands it on its head. Seeing this dark content injected into a sitcom format makes the subject matter even more repulsive. The scene is highly effective because it welcomes us in with a familiar format, then shows us things we don't want to see.

Script Note

In the script excerpt the flashback belongs to Mickey, Mallory's boyfriend. In the final film, the flashback is given to Mallory.

Natural Born Killers (1994) (Page 48)

INT. MALLORY'S PARENTS' LIVING ROOM - NIGHT - FLASHBACK

The set is sitcom TV format. The lighting is flat, the performances and timing are TV. It is SHOT in three camera SITCOM FORMAT -- possibly BLACK and WHITE, harkening back to an earlier era in Mickey's mind. The time when he first saw TV.

*(Mickey's VO Omitted)

MALLORY gets a big handful of AUDIENCE APPLAUSE as she comes down the stairs, dressed to the nines, punky, sexy, ready to trot -- yet a sweet girl's expression, maybe with braces.

MALLORY

Hello Dad, how was work?

DAD is a strange-looking hombre, seated at the table, exhausted and angry in a dirty undershirt.

DAD

Work? What work! I'm unemployed. Three years.
I'm unemployed.

(LAUGHTRACK)

MOM is always-smiling with cracked-egg eyes, serving him a large salt cracker with pea soup.

MOM

You look nice, Mallory.

Her younger brother, KEVIN, is doing his homework at the table.

KEVIN

Yuck. She looks like...uccckkk.

(LAUGHTRACK)

MALLORY (IGNORING KEVIN)

Thanks Mom. I'm late. I'll be back by midnight.

DAD

What are you wearing? A broom stick in a trash
bag. A few pounds lighter and you'd be Miss
Ethiopia. Where the hell do you think you're
going?

MALLORY

To the John Lee Hooker concert. With Donna. I
told you yesterday.

Dad rises and tracks her across the living room. She's evidently not going anywhere tonight in his mind.

DAD

First off, you don't tell me anything, you ask
my permission. Second, you can't go out in
that whorehouse dress. Third, you can't go out
at all. You didn't mow the yard.

3.

2.

1.

4.

82. Film Element: Candlelight

Candlelight has a number of important properties. It flatters the face, smoothes the skin, and adds a warm tone. It suggests romance, festivities, and harmony. It is also linked historically with the pre-twentieth century. Stanley Kubrick, in trying to stay true to his period piece, *Barry Lyndon*, filmed the entire movie using only candlelight and natural light.

In the example below the conventions usually associated with candlelight are sabotaged to show us the underbelly of a suburban family.

Film Example: *American Beauty*

To show the dysfunction of his protagonist's family life, writer Alan Ball exploits the properties usually associated with candlelight. When we first arrive at Lestor's (Kevin Spacey) family dinner scene, it appears harmonious. The table is lit with candles, lending a warm and harmonious glow to the symmetrical image. The table is elegant and the lighting is almost too romantic for a family dinner.

However, as soon as the characters begin to speak, we realize that the family dynamics are far from harmonious. These characters are probably more appropriately positioned under the florescent lights of divorce court. The candlelight mocks Lestor's wife's (Annette Bening) attempt to create a picture-perfect life. The romantic setting also underscores what both husband and wife have lost over the course of their marriage.

Dramatic Value

By subverting the traditional associations of candlelight, writer Alan Ball is able to show the audience how far from the idealized life Lestor and his family have traveled.

Other Films

Barry Lyndon

The English Patient

American Beauty (1999)
Page 17)

Screenplay: Alan Ball, 4/1/98.

INT. BURNHAM HOUSE - DINING ROOM - LATER
THAT NIGHT

We HEAR John Coltrane and Johnny
Hartman's rendition of "YOU
ARE TOO BEAUTIFUL" on the STEREO.

LESTER, Carolyn and JANE are seated at
dinner IN the formaldining room. They
eat by CANDLELIGHT, and a profusion
of RED ROSES spills from a vase at the
center of the table. We CIRCLE them
slowly, as they eat. Nobody makes eye
contact, or even seems aware of anybody
else's presence, until...

83. Film Element: Motivated Lighting

Motivated lighting refers to any light that would naturally exist in the world depicted in the frame. The source of light might be a lamp post that shines light on a couple, but is not itself depicted in the scene. Or it could be a lamp that appears on screen.

Film Example: *Fatal Attraction*

In *Fatal Attraction* Eve (Glen Close) has become increasingly more dangerous to her lover and herself. Not able to convince Dan (Michael Douglas) to continue their relationship, Close attempts suicide. Soon after, Douglas rejects her invitation to see *Madame Butterfly* — on the night of the scheduled performance, Close listens to a recording of the opera at home alone. As she does, she turns a nearby lamp on and off continuously.

Dramatic Value

The action, and the effect of the light, suggest the intermittent nature of her sanity, and mirrors the highs and lows she experiences emotionally. The use of light is remarkable in its simplicity, especially when you consider the complexity of its meaning and the immediacy with which we understand it. All is delivered by nothing more than the on-and-off switch from an ordinary lamp.

1.

2.

3.

84. Film Element: Unmotivated Light

Light is traditionally used as a symbol representing moral goodness, darkness as evil. In Luc Besson's brilliant film, *The Professional*, Besson uses unmotivated light to recalibrate expected assumptions about his protagonist, Leon, a professional assassin.

Film Example: *The Professional*

At the end of Act One, we see a young girl's family being slaughtered by corrupt cops. The young girl, who was absent, returns home to see her young brother dead in the open door of her apartment. Knowing she will be killed if she identifies herself, she walks past her brother to her neighbor's door. Her neighbor is already known to us as a professional assassin and recluse.

After much internal struggle, the assassin throws open the door to the young girl. The girl becomes bathed in light. The source of light cannot be logically explained, giving the scene an almost religious quality. In being associated with an inexplicable flood of light, especially one of this power, the assassin becomes morally recalibrated for the audience.

Dramatic Value

Characterizing a professional assassin as a positive moral force is a difficult job. Besson uses unmotivated light to help the audience reset their moral compass.

Script Note

Besson, who was both writer and director of the film, added "the bath of light" later in the film's development. Nonetheless, the script beautifully sets up the opportunity.

The Professional (Léon) (1994) (Scene 19, Page 15)

Screenplay: Luc Besson. Draft: Seaside 1993. Slugline below added for clarity.

```
INT. HALLWAY

The GIRL, carrying two very large bags of groceries, comes up the
stairs.
She slows her steps.

She immediately senses something's wrong.
LEON'S worried about her.

MALKY watches her approach.
Looking down as always, the girl sees the feet of her dead father as
one of the men drags his body through the hallway. Without breaking
her stride or looking up, she walks past her apartment as if nothing
has happened.

She pretends not to notice MALKY, who is still guarding the
apartment door.
She goes to the end of the hallway, stops in front of LEON's door,
and rings the buzzer.
Tears start to roll down her cheeks.
MALKY is still watching her.
Now Leon is really worried. He doesn't know what to do.

Finally LEON opens the door. The girl enters without a word.
```

1.

2.

3.

85. Film Element: Motion

A moving light can be created in a number of ways. In *Metropolis* it's a man with an oil lamp, in *Psycho* it's a swinging bare light bulb, and in *ET* it's men with flashlights.

In all three cases a moving light evokes fear. In *ET* and *Metropolis* it's because the moving light represents an approaching antagonist. When a light source is carried, it has an unpredictable quality. In this way it can imply anything from chaos to madness. Our fear can also be progressively heightened as a moving light can suggest the closing of the gap between antagonist and protagonist.

In *Psycho*, however, our fear stems from being disoriented. When we first see the swinging light bulb, we don't know what we're seeing. Although it can do us no harm, we are afraid of it until our eyes can adjust and identify the object.

Each of these moving lights can equally represent safety. A flashlight and oil lamp can rescue, and an electric light can silence our fear of the dark. However, when light moves chaotically, we naturally fear it. All three of these films use this conventional response to evoke fear. Here's the setup in *ET*.

Film Example: *ET*

In the opening pages of *ET*, ET is pursued by humans who are immediately identified as ET's antagonists. They arrive in big trucks with huge beaming headlights. Once they emerge from the vehicles, they switch light sources; they now pursue ET with the aid of powerful flashlights.

The chaotic beams of light produced by the gang of faceless men work well to pique our fears.

Dramatic Value

The chaotic movement of light naturally sets off fear in the audience. It can be exploited to raise our sympathies for the protagonist. Moving light can also be romantic as in *The English Patient* where flickering candlelight is used. Much depends on the nature of the movement and the scene content.

Other Films

Psycho   (climax scene with a swinging bulb)

Metropolis   (innocent heroine pursued by a scientist aided by an oil lamp)

ET (1982) (Scene 26, Page 5)

Screenplay: Melissa Mathison, Rev. Sept. 8, 1981,
Shooting Script.

26. WIDER: MORE CARS

More cars converge on the scene. We SEE bright
HEADLIGHTS and HEAR slamming doors, muffled voices.
Then we HEAR the creature break a branch from a
shrub. He holds it against his chest. The SOUND of
KEYS.

The sudden shafts of flashlight beams encircle the
road and shoot out into the trees.

The CREATURE moves unnoticed along the hillside.
He crosses the road.

27. EXT. RAVINE - NIGHT - LONG SHOT

We see shadows of men jumping the ravine and
heading into the forest. The CREATURE hides in the
near end of the shallow ravine.

KEYS is the last to jump.

The SOUND of KEYS is hideous.

1.

2.

3.

4.

Chapter Credits By Film Element

80. *Apocalypse Now* (1979)
Writer: John Milius (Screenplay) &
Writer: Francis Coppola (Screenplay)
Writer: Joseph Conrad (Uncredited)
Director: Francis Coppola
Production Company: Zoetrope
Distributor: United Artists

81. *Natural Born Killers* (1994)
Writer: David Veloz (Screenplay) &
Writer   Richard Rutowski (Screenplay) &
Writer: Oliver Stone (Screenplay)
Writer: Quentin Tarantino (Story)
Director: Oliver Stone
Production Company: Alcor Films
Production Company: Ixtlan Productions
Production Company: JD Productions
Production Company: New Regency Pictures
Production Company: Regency Enterprises
Production Company: Warner Brothers
Distributor: Warner Home Video (USA) (DVD)
Note: Writing credits on the script excerpted for this book, called Draft Five, May 11, 1993, were: Quentin Tarantino, David Veloz, Richard Rutowski, and Oliver Stone. In the final film credits, Quentin Tarantino received "story" credit.

82. *American Beauty* (1999)
Writer: Alan Ball
Director: Sam Mendes
Production Company: Dreamworks SKG
Production Company: Jinks/Cohen Company
Distributor: Dreamworks

83. *Fatal Attraction* (1987)
Writer: James Dearden (Screenplay) (also earlier version)
Writer: Nicholas Meyer
Director: Adrian Lyne
Production Company: Paramount Pictures
Distributor: Paramount Home Video (USA) (DVD)

84. *The Professional* (1994)
Writer: Luc Besson (Screenplay)
Director: Luc Besson
Production Company: Gaumont International
Production Company: Les Films du Dauphin
Distributor: Columbia TriStar Home Video (USA) (DVD)

85. *ET* (1982)
Writer: Melissa Mathison (Screenplay)
Director: Steven Spielberg
Production Company: Amblin Entertainment
Production Company: Universal Pictures
Distributor: Columbia TriStar Home Video (USA) (DVD)

SECTION 13

COLOR

86. Film Element: Coding Character

Robert Altman has described his 1977 film *Three Women* as a story about "identity theft" (Altman). Each of his female characters steals identities as they need them. We are able to measure their success as each character is given a signature color: Pinkie Rose is Pink; Millie is Yellow; and Willie is the color of sand. As each woman steals the identity of the other, she also appropriates her color. Here's how one of the transformations was represented.

Pinkie Rose (Sissy Spacek) enters the film wearing a pale flesh color. She is like a blank canvas in search of a livable identity. After each tragic event, she transforms, taking over another character's color and persona. Her transformations are ongoing and occur like movements in music.

1. Pinkie Rose arrives at a desert spa, like a character without a past, in a pink girlish dress. Here Pinkie meets Millie (Shelley Duvall) who becomes her idol.

2. Pinkie takes over Millie's persona and becomes identified with Millie's "yellow."

3. After surviving a coma, Pinkie rejects Millie and returns to pink, only this time it's hot pink. Pinkie's clothing goes from girlish to sexual.

4. Finally, after back-to-back tragedies, Pinkie returns to her former clothing. Only this time the pink appears sun-bleached and even further muted. Both Pinkie and Millie have entered Willie's world of desert colors. Both have found personas that heal themselves and Willie. Pinkie has become Willie's grandchild, and Millie her daughter. We are left with the feeling that this final transformation is a just a temporary resting point.

Dramatic Value

Color is used to identify each character's initial persona. Later it is used to externalize the theft of another character's persona and to indicate how far along the characters are in their transformation.

Other Films

Body Heat (color changes in Kathleen Turner's wardrobe)

Reservoir Dogs (naming of characters by color)

1.

2.

3.

4.

Chapter Credits By Film Element

86. *Three Women* (1977)
Writer: Robert Altman (Screenplay)
Writer: Patricia Resnick (Uncredited)
Director: Robert Altman
Production Company: Lions Gate Films
Distributor: 20th Century Fox Film Corporation
Distributor: Criterion Collection (2004) USA (DVD)

87. Film Element: Props (Externalizing Character)

Props provide a dramatic way to express a character's inner world. Props speak visually, are mobile, and can be returned to throughout the movie.

Film Example: *Barton Fink*

Here's how the Coen Brothers use props to introduce Barton to his new hotel room. Each prop becomes iconic and reappears later in the film.

1. The squeaky bed.	When Barton enters, he tosses his suitcase on the bed. The bed springs squeak unusually loudly. It's as though the sound track is signaling that the bed is going to be important. Later Barton finds a dead woman in it.
2. The sealed window	When Barton tries the window, it too comments. The window is stuck, like Barton. Barton can't leave until his story is done.
3. The typewriter	The typewriter is introduced with a close-up. We hold on it because it represents the movie's central conflict.
4. The pad of paper	On the desk, there is a pad with Hotel Earle's logo and tagline, "A Day or a Lifetime." This implied question becomes more important as the film goes on.
5. Pencil	When Barton moves the pencil on the pad, the paper beneath it is white, the paper around it yellowed. Unlike Barton, no one has used a pencil in his room for years. This underscores that writers are outsiders in the Hotel Earle. Later when Barton brings a writer to his room she is killed.
6. The postcard	The girl on the postcard is Barton's muse, a fantasy projection. Again the sound track tells us this is important by laying crashing waves and gulls beneath the image.

Dramatic Value

Each of the props represents important ideas in the movie, and each is returned to later.

Script Note

Barton's action, moving the pencil that reveals the yellowed stationery, is in the movie, but not in this draft of the script. Barton's interaction with the window also differs slightly.

Barton Fink (1991)

Screenplay: Joel Coen & Ethan Coen, Feb. 19, 1990.

```
HIS ROOM

As Barton enters.

The room is small and cheaply furnished. There is a lumpy
bed with a worn-yellow coverlet, an old secretary table,
and a wooden luggage stand.

As Barton crosses the room we follow to reveal a sink and
wash basin, a house telephone on a rickety night stand,
and a window with yellowing sheers looking on an air
shaft.

Barton throws his valise onto the bed where it sinks,
jittering. He shrugs off his jacket.

Pips of sweat stand out on Barton's brow. The room is hot.

He walks across the room, switches on an oscillating fan
and struggles to throw open the window. After he strains
at it for a moment, it slides open with a great wrenching
sound.

Barton picks up his Underwood and places it on the
secretary table. He gives the machine a casually
affectionate pat.

Next to the typewriter are a few sheets of house
stationary: THE HOTEL EARLE: A DAY OR A LIFETIME.

We pan up to a picture in a cheap wooden frame on the wall
above the desk.

A bathing beauty sits on the beach under a cobalt blue
sky. One hand shields her eyes from the sun as she looks
out at a crashing surf.

The sound of the surf mixes up.

BARTON

Looking at the picture

TRACKING IN ON THE PICTURE

The surf mixes up louder. We hear a gull cry.

The sound snaps off with the ring of a telephone.
```

1.

4.

2.

5.

3.

88. Film Element: Props (Externalizing Character)

Purposely selecting and exploiting *props* can give a scene an added layer of meaning. Film classics like *Citizen Kane, Chinatown, and One Flew Over the Cuckoo's Nest* offer brilliant illustrations of their use. The following example is from *Raging Bull*, one of the best films of the 1980s, where a single prop is able to translate the increasing mental instability of its protagonist.

Film Example: *Raging Bull*

By midpoint in the movie, prizefighter Jake La Motta has begun to lose his way. He is increasingly paranoid of all those around him. In this scene Jake is at home adjusting the picture of his TV. At first the TV signal is intermittent, as is Jake's sanity. When Jake's wife enters and kisses Jake's brother on the cheek, Jake's paranoia is set off. Now the TV goes completely haywire.

The television picture is brilliantly used to convey Jake's escalating mental agitation which culminates in Jake's beating both his wife and brother. The final scene in the sequence returns to Jake in front of the TV. The TV again mirrors his mental state. Now Jake sits like a rag doll, completely drained and alone, staring at the screen, which now pictures nothing but scrolling horizontal lines.

Dramatic Value

Here a prop is put to use to graphically illustrate a character's changing mental state. As the prop is organic to the scene, it is able to add to the other layers of story, such as dialog and action, without calling attention to itself.

Other Films

Citizen Kane
Chinatown
One Flew Over the Cuckoo's Nest
Bound
The Professional
Harold and Maude
American Beauty
Blade Runner

Raging Bull (1980) (Page 67)

Screenplay: Paul Shrader and Mardik Martin.

```
INT. JAKE'S LIVING ROOM - DAY (1950)

JAKE is struggling with his later model ten-inch
RCA TV. He fools with the dials, then slaps the
side. The bluish video image comes and goes. JOEY
watches JAKE fix the TV.

JAKE has a half-eaten sandwich in his hand.
VICKIE enters the house, surprised to find JAKE home.
                    VICKIE
            Jake, you're home.

JAKE looks up at her. (She goes over to him and
kisses him.) MOVING SHOT.

JOEY gives VICKIE a polite peck on the mouth.
MOVING SHOT.

                    JOEY
            Hi, Vickie.

JAKE watches JOEY kiss VICKIE. VICKIE notices
JAKE'S reaction.

                    VICKIE
            What's the matter with you?

                    JAKE
            Tryin' to get this fuckin' TV to
            work. Paid all this money for it
            and still can't get a station a
            mile away. And Mr. Wizard here
            ain't no help.

                    JOEY
            Screw you, Jack.

                    JAKE
                (to Vickie)

            Where you been?

VICKIE goes into the bedroom to take off her coat.
On the stairs, MOVING SHOT:

                    VICKIE
            I went out.

                    JAKE
                (to Joey)

            What's that kissing on the mouth shit?
```

1.

2.

3.

4.

5.

89. Film Element: Repurposing Props

Props, like wardrobe, live alongside the characters in a movie. Writers can leave them silent, or use them to give further depth to their characters and plot.

Repurposing props is when the meaning of a prop changes over the course of the movie. For example, a prop might mean "hope" in Act One, "imprisonment" in Act Two, and "hope" again in Act Three. Props provide the writer and director with another way of indicating ideas on screen. Creating a progression of meaning can add subtext and depth to the more obvious outer story.

Film Example: *Bound*

In this brilliant noir love triangle, garden clippers are used by the mob in Act One to dismember one their own for stealing (Image 1).

Later in the film, one of the main characters, Ceasar, who is also a mobster, borrows the technique to threaten his wife and his wife's lover, Corky (Image 2-3).

But at the end of the film, Corky, who has become Ceasar's next victim, frees herself with the same clippers (Image 4).

The writers could have had Corky free herself in a number of ways. By returning to the same clippers, already branded with a specific meaning, the writers can show story progression. When Corky succeeds, the clippers represent a shift in power.

Dramatic Value

By returning to iconic props already used, change can be shown. In this way we can measure where we are in a film. Adding new props along the way is relatively easy. Mining props from earlier scenes is tougher and far more powerful.

Other Films

The Professional (Léon's house plant)

1.

2.

3.

4.

90. Film Element: Contrast

A movie's theme will naturally suggest images to the writer. In Altman's *Three Women* color is central, in *Ed Wood*, wardrobe, and in *Harold and Maude*, vehicles.

Film Example: *Harold and Maude*

In some movies people drive off in "cars," "sedans," and "vans," but in *Harold and Maude* the vehicle world is specific.

Harold's fascination with death is represented by his home-made "hearse," formerly a Jaguar.

Maude has also redefined a vehicle. She has taken a railway car and turned it into her home. The choice of a railway car becomes especially significant when later we learn she has been in a concentration camp.

Other vehicle choices are also carefully made. When Harold and Maude steal a car, it's a Lincoln Continental, and when his uncle shows Harold around, they travel in a chauffeur-driven limousine. Each character is given a signature vehicle. Harold's final liberation and the climax in the movie, shows Harold sending his "hearse" off a cliff. Harold gives up his "hearse" so he can embrace the living.

Dramatic Value

Like wardrobe or hand props, vehicles can be an important tool to differentiate characters. As always how to externalize ideas is determined by story value.

Other Films

Three Women

Ed Wood

Harold and Maude (1971)

Screenplay: Colin Higgins.

Here are three script excerpts demonstrating how Colin Higgins put vehicles to use in his script.

113.   MRS. CHASEN'S POV

Harold is putting the final polish on the car. The car, however, has changed. It is now black, with a squared off top, a long back, black velvet curtains, and silver trim.

As Edith says...

> EDITH
> Oh it looks like a hearse.
>
> (a pause)
>
> Very nice. Compact.

127D. INT. UNCLE VICTOR'S CAR - DAY

Uncle Victor and Harold are seated in the back of the general's military limousine. As they ride along, Uncle Victor is being very expansive. Harold is being unusually attentive.

194. EXT. THE PROMONTORY - EXTREME LONG SHOT - DAY

The little hearse falls from the cliff, crashing at the bottom, and bursting into flames.

Note: First column of images corresponds to script excerpts.
Second column of images are other examples of vehicles used for characterization.

1.

2.

3.

4.

5.

6.

Chapter Credits By Film Element

87. *Barton Fink* (1991)
Writer:	Joel Coen (Screenplay) &
Writer:	Ethan Coen (Screenplay)
Director:	Joel Coen
Director:	Ethan Coen (Uncredited)
Production Company:	Circle Films Inc.
Production Company:	Working Title Films
Distributor:	20th Century Fox Film Corporation

88. *Raging Bull* (1980)
Writer:	Paul Shrader (Screenplay) and
Writer:	Mardik Martin (Screenplay)
Writer:	Jake La Motta (Book) and
Writer:	Joseph Carter (Book) &
Writer:	Peter Savage (Book)
Director:	Martin Scorsese
Production Company:	Chartoff-Winkler Productions
Distributor:	United Artists
Distributor:	MGM Home Entertainment (USA) (DVD)

89. *Bound* (1996)
Writer:	The Wachowski Brothers & The Wachowski Brothers
Director:	The Wachowski Brothers & The Wachowski Brothers
Production Company:	Dino de Laurentiis Productions
Production Company:	Spelling Films
Distributor:	Gramercy Pictures

90. *Harold and Maude* (1971)
Writer:	Colin Higgins (Screenplay)
Director:	Hal Ashby
Production Company:	Paramount Pictures
Distributor:	Paramount Pictures

SECTION **15**

WARDROBE

91. Film Element: Wardrobe

The decision to include a *wardrobe* element in a script depends on whether it adds sufficient dramatic value. In films where wardrobe is central to the character, like *Hedwig and the Angry Inch, Cabaret, Single White Female,* or *Three Women,* the writer will most likely create a wardrobe continuum. To make the point, there were over 200 wardrobe references *in Ed Wood,* a film where the main character was a cross-dresser and a film director. Here wardrobe references for the protagonist and other actors were dynamically used. In other movies, other elements are more important.

Film Example: *Ed Wood*

In the brilliant script written by Scott Alexander and Larry Karaszewski, Ed Wood's cross-dressing is central to the story. What makes the script especially intriguing is that the cross-dressing is not just used sensationally. The writers show us how it works in the character's psyche. In a pivotal scene, Ed enters the dressing room of a movie set completely distraught. Then we see him "self-medicate" and return to the set, calm and fully in control. Ed's "self-medication" begins when he rubs an angora sweater he's found in the dressing room. When he returns to the set he is wearing women's clothing, including the sweater. Where some people need a cigarette or a drink, Ed needs angora. It's a wonderful scene.

Dramatic Value

The wardrobe choices in *Ed Wood* are purposefully used to externalize the inner workings of the character. They work beautifully contributing to characterization and the tone of the movie.

Other Films

Cabaret

Hedwig and the Angry Inch

Single White Female

Ed Wood (1994)

Screenplay: Scott Alexander & Larry Karaszewski, First Draft:
Nov. 20, 1992. Based on the book by Rudolph Grey.

```
INT. DRESSING ROOM - SAME TIME

Ed bursts in. Hysterically traumatized.

                    ED
          They're driving me crazy! These Baptists are
          stupid, stupid, STUPID.

Ed glances at a clothing rack -- and sees an ANGORA
SWEATER.

Ed is taken aback. He slowly removes it from the hanger
and rubs it against his face. His breathing slows.

                    ED
          Mmm... I need to calm... Take deep breaths...

               (he rubs the angora)

          Ohh, it's so smooth....

INT. SOUNDSTAGE - SAME TIME

The dressing room door flies open. Ed slowly struts out,
in the sweater, pantsuit, and pumps. He is calmed and at
ease.
```

1.

2.

3.

92. Film Element: Repurposing Wardrobe

For most writers and directors externalizing a character's change is a problem, especially if they don't want to rely on dialog. The use of an iconic wardrobe element can be very useful in showing change over time.

The key is to set up the wardrobe element in Act One, then revisit it over the course of the movie. Here's how screenwriter Kurt Luedtke used a simple pair of gloves to tell us about Karen von Blixen's transformation in *Out of Africa*.

Film Example: *Out of Africa*

At the beginning of the film, protagonist Karen von Blixen is portrayed as a woman who has married for an aristocratic title. She values the trappings of European aristocracy and fights to bring these things to her farm in Africa. They include fine china and furniture. She also tries to run her household like one in Europe. When she hires a young African boy, Juma, she has him wear a pair of white gloves emulating the uniform of European servants.

Inspired by the country and her lover, Denys, Karen begins to transform. Finally at the end of the film she removes Juma's gloves. In freeing him, she has also freed herself.

Dramatic Value

By setting up the first "glove scene" in Act One, the audience can refer back to the scene over the course of the movie and measure change. By the end of the movie, when Karen removes Juma's gloves, the meaning is clear.

Other Films

Thelma and Louise

Single White Female

Out of Africa (1985)

Screenplay: Kurt Luedke, August 1983 version. See Chapter Credits.

INT/DINING ROOM-DAY (First Use Page 27)

```
Karen puts white gloves on Juma, buttons them for him. He
holds his hands as though they were broken.
```

Further down the same page--

```
INT/DINING ROOM-NIGHT

She's alone with her dinner, reading by a kerosene lamp.
As Juma clears, a plate slips from his hands; he looks
helplessly at his gloves.
```

A SERIES OF SHOTS (Later Use)

```
--AT DINNER. Karen's in a gown, Denys in a burnoose,
Berkeley in shorts and Bror's dinner jacket, too large.
The table's elegant, her best things; both Farrah and Juma
serve while Esa fusses at the door. Denys and Juma joke over
Juma's gloves. Karen watches Denys, contemplative.
```

INT/DINING ROOM-NIGHT (Final Use Page 125)

```
The room is nearly bare, much as it was when she first came.
The candelabra is gone: stubby candles light the table.
They've dressed for dinner; her gown is long but she wears
no jewelry and no makeup. Juna pours coffee, would retire,
but:

                    KAREN
          Juma? Take off those silly gloves.

A broad smile. He removes them, leaves them on the table.
She smokes, looks around the room.

                    KAREN
          We should have had it this way all
          the time.
```

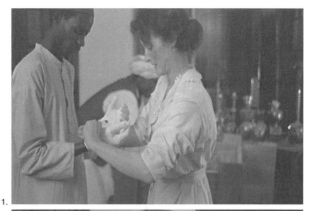

1.

2.

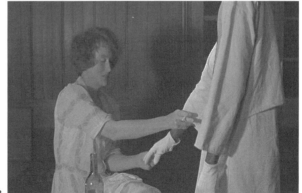

3.

93. Film Element: Contrast of Wardrobe

In the previous example, wardrobe was used to show character transformation. In the Wachowski Brothers' *Bound*, *contrast of wardrobe* is used to differentiate the two female leads.

Film Example: *Bound*

Both women in this *noir* thriller are outsiders. Violet is a prostitute by trade, and Corky, a thief. And both wear their professions on their ears. Violet wears long dangling earrings designed for seduction. Corky's earrings, on the other hand, are silver lockpicks, worn for easy access.

Dramatic Value

Wardrobe can be subtle or more obvious. It can show similarity, contrast, irony, discomfort, poverty, or wealth, for example. In *Bound* it is wonderfully used to show contrast.

Other Films

Single White Female (contrast and parallel)

Thelma and Louise (change)

Harold and Maude (parallel — psychiatrist's office)

Bound (1996)

Screenplay: Larry Wachowski & Andy Wachowski, Draft: Sept. 28, 1994

Page 13: Violet's Earrings: Source of Seduction

INT. CEASAR'S APARTMENT

Violet leads her through the apartment. It is expensively
furnished with very masculine tastes; a lot of gray and
black leather.

>   VIOLET
>   I was doing some dishes and just
>   as I pulled the stopper my earring fell in.

Corky looks at her blankly.

>   VIOLET
>   It's one of my favorites. That's why
>   I got upset. I know it probably seems
>   ridiculous to you.

Page 53: Corky's Earrings: Lock Picks as Tools of the Trade

INT. OFFICE

The black case is lying on the desk, locked shut. Corky
moves around the desk, dropping down behind it.

>   CORKY (V.O)
>   When I'm inside, I will get the money.

From her ear-lobe she chooses the right pick, sliding out a
silver tool.

It takes only a second and the first lock pops.

Chapter Credits By Film Element

91. *Ed Wood* (1994)

Writer:	Scott Alexander (Screenplay) &
Writer:	Larry Karaszewski (Screenplay
Writer:	Rudolph Grey (Book: *Nightmare of Ecstasy*)
Director:	Tim Burton
Production Company:	Touchstone Pictures
Distributor:	Buena Vista

92. *Out of Africa* (1985)

Writer:	Kurt Luedtke (Screenplay)
Writer:	Isak Dinesen (Memoirs)
Writer:	A.E. Housman (Poem: "To an Athlete, Dying Young" (Uncredited)
Writer:	Errol Trzebinski (Book: *Silence will Speak*)
Director:	Sydney Pollack
Production Company:	Mirage Entertainment
Distributor:	MCA/Universal Pictures

93. *Bound* (1996)

Writer:	The Wachowski Brothers & The Wachowski Brothers
Director:	The Wachowski Brothers & The Wachowski Brothers
Production Company:	Dino de Laurentiis Productions
Production Company:	Spelling Films
Distributor:	Gramercy Pictures

SECTION **16**

LOCATIONS

94. Film Element: Defining Character

One of the difficulties in any film is how to externalize the inner thoughts of a character. This is especially true when there is no narrator to rely on for exposition.

Location is especially important to learn how to exploit, as it's available in every shot. Two films that fully harness its dramatic potential are *Hedwig and the Angry Inch* and *The Sweet Hereafter*. Here's how it was put to use in *Hedwig and the Angry Inch*.

Film Example: *Hedwig and the Angry Inch*

In *Hedwig and the Angry Inch* a young man struggles with his conflicted sexuality. His struggle is set against the backdrop of Berlin, a city divided in half.

Dramatic Value

The metaphor of a divided city works brilliantly to express Hedwig's divided self.

Script Note

The script excerpt, on the accompanying page, includes the lyrics sung by the protagonist in the movie's opening scene. The frame grabs are images throughout the movie that depict the use of Berlin as a metaphor.

Hedwig and the Angry Inch (2001)

Screenplay and Play: John Cameron Mitchell; Play music
& lyrics: Stephen Trask. Draft: Revised 1/30/00.

Opening Lyrics sung by Hedwig, the protagonist.

> I'm the new Berlin Wall
> Try to tear me down
>
> Standing before you
> On a divide between
> East and West
> Slavery and Freedom
> Man and Woman

Animation Sequences and Artwork by Emily Hubley

1.

2.

3.

4.

5.

95. Film Element: Location as Unifying Element

As film is a visual medium, location offers a huge storytelling potential. It can heighten drama, suggest parallels and contrast, and help define character. It can also take us to places where we have never been before. And it can do it wordlessly. In Atom Egoyan's moving film, location is meticulously used to unify his characters.

Film Example: *The Sweet Hereafter*

The Sweet Hereafter is a drama set in a small town during a bleak Canadian winter. A tragedy strikes when the local school bus crashes into the water and most of the town's children die. Mitch, a city lawyer, soon arrives. His object is to encourage the parents to focus their anger on the bus manufacturer by participating in a law suit.

While Mitch deals with the town's overwhelming loss, he comes to face to face with his own: the loss of his teenage daughter to heroin addiction.

Like Mitch, each of the main characters is identified with a similar location: a rectangular, enclosed box, shaped like a coffin. The use of the coffin imagery throughout the film never lets us forget the loss at the core of the story — the rectangular bus that held the children.

When we first meet Mitch he drives into a dark car wash. He is encased both in the car wash and in his car. Both rectangular shapes. The pouring water imprisons him in his vehicle. Later, we will understand how this opening image parallels the image of the children in the water-submerged bus.

While inside the car, Mitch receives a phone call from his drug-addicted daughter, Zoe. We then cut to Zoe inside a windowed phone booth. The phone both visually mimics Mitch's location and underscores the physical separation between them. As Mitch becomes more upset, the water cycle finishes, leaving water trickling down Mitch's windows like tears.

Dramatic Value

By coding the rectangular, coffin-like locations as symbols of death, Egoyan can thematically connect the characters. Although the town's grieving parents, Mitch, and his daughter all appear to be separated by circumstances, they all carry death with them.

Other Films

Thelma and Louise

Blade Runner

Blue Velvet

The Sweet Hereafter (1997) (Scene 2)

Screenplay: Atom Egoyan, Final Revised Draft, 1997. Based on the novel by Russell Banks.

```
INT./EXT. CAR WASH -- NIGHT
```

From the peaceful tableau of the sleeping family, the scene shifts to a vehicle entering a car wash. The image is shot through the windshield, from the driver's point of view.

The car enters the lathered world of spinning felt wheels and gushing water.

```
CUT TO:

INT. CAR WASH -- NIGHT
```

Inside the car MITCHELL STEPHENS, a man in his mid-fifties, listens to a stirring piece of music. The sound of the car wash is filtered out by the strains of music.

```
CUT TO:

EXT. PHONE BOOTH -- NIGHT
```

The phone booth is located in a rundown area of a large city. A young woman, ZOE, enters the booth and lifts the receiver.

```
CUT TO:

INT. CAR WASH -- NIGHT
```

MITCHELL STEPHENS is going through the wash. The automatic mops and buffers embrace his car with water and suds. The cellular phone in the car rings. MITCHELL picks it up.

```
                    MITCHELL
          Yes? Yes, I'll accept the charges.

CUT TO:

INT. PHONE BOOTH -- NIGHT
```

ZOE is on the phone. There's a figure outside the booth waiting for her.

1.

2.

3.

4.

96. Film Element: Location as Theme

A well-crafted film uses everything to contribute to story. There are no throwaways, and location is no exception. Here's how David Lynch put location to work in setting up the theme in his brilliant film, *Blue Velvet*.

Film Example: *Blue Velvet*

Blue Velvet opens in a perfect suburb. An iconic homeowner waters his lawn as a smiling fireman drives by. We then cut to fresh-faced children crossing a crosswalk on the way to school. Everything seems as it should be.

Once we absorb this idealized view, the film sabotages our expectations. The film now returns us to the iconic man watering his lawn. This time there is a kink in the hose. Suddenly, the man is stung by an insect which causes some kind of seizure. A moment later he lies dead on his freshly watered lawn as a diapered infant approaches.

The camera now descends past the blades of grass, down to the dirt below and finally, to a mass of insects "crawling and scratching" in the dark. Once we have time to be repulsed, we are returned to the surface. Once again we are given a suburban icon of wellness — a brightly colored billboard depicting a pretty suburban mom welcoming the viewer. Underneath her image of suburban propriety we read: "Welcome to Lumberton."

Dramatic Value

The writer establishes suburban normalcy carefully with a number of iconic shots. When he shows us the underbelly of the town, we have a standard against which to measure the deviation. He does this through camera reveals and by revisiting the same characters. This scene cleverly sets up the theme through location. The opening scene warns us not to accept superficial perfection because everything has an underbelly. The rest of the film convinces us.

Script Note

We come in on page two. This is the last scene creating the idyllic suburbs. Then the view shifts to show us the underbelly of the suburb.

Other Films

American Beauty (idealized suburban)

Blue Velvet (1986) (Scene 6, Page 2)

Screenplay: David Lynch Final script.

6. EXT. BEAUMONTS' FRONT LAWN - DAY

PANNING SLOWLY now away from the roses down to the rich green
lawn and over to the sprinkler which goes around and around
shooting water droplets sparkling in the light.

This is slightly SLOW MOTION and DREAMY.

DISSOLVE TO:

7. EXT. BEAUMONTS' FRONT LAWN - DAY

CLOSER ON WATER DROPLETS. The water droplets are somewhat
abstracted as they dance in the light.

PAN DOWN now to the green grass, traveling along the grass.

The MUSIC becomes fainter as we MOVE SUDDENLY under the
grass, now as if in a dark forest.

SLOWLY MOVING THROUGH.

The grass is like great timbers.

It is GETTING DARKER and ominous SOUNDS come up as we
discover black insects crawling and scratching in the
darkness.

FADE TO:

8. EXT. BEAUMONT'S FRONT LAWN - DAY

MR. BEAUMONT is watering flowers and grass with the hose.

He is dressed in khaki trousers, canvas shoes, old white
shirt, straw hat and dark glasses.

CLOSE - MR. BEAUMONT

watches his watering, then looks up.

The sky and the neighborhood are reflected in his dark
glasses. He moves his false teeth around a little in his
mouth, jutting out his chin in the process. He's thinking
about who knows what.

He looks back down at his lawn.

97. Film Element: Moving Locations

Film Element: Moving Locations

Road trip movies are especially adept at using the changing landscape to externalize conflict and character. Jim Jarmusch's beautiful black-and-white film *Dead Man* sets up character and story by an extended opening montage that features a changing landscape.

Film Example: *Dead Man*

Jim Jarmusch's *Dead Man*, set in the 1800s, traces the demise of a young accountant who travels from Cleveland to the Western town of Machine. Jarmusch sets up the movie's dark tone in a ten-minute opening montage. The montage shows the changing landscape as his protagonist's train heads to the edges of the western frontier. Each cut shows us a more forbidding landscape along with a new set of passengers, each rougher than the previous set. By the last cut, the fur-clad passengers shoot buffalo out the window of the moving train for sport. A threshold character, who appears mad, warns the protagonist, William Blake, that there is no job waiting for him, and the town of Machine is the "end of the line."

The "moving landscape" takes us from civilization to lawless frontier, where the fragile William Blake will meet his end. The "moving landscape" sets up the story and foreshadows the protagonist's death.

Other Films

Thelma and Louise

Dead Man (Page 1)

Screenplay: Jim Jarmusch, Draft 2/21/1994.

INT. TRAIN - DAY

Moving lights flicker across the lids of CLOSED EYES. Gradually the eyes open, emerging from sleep. They blink drowsily, then shift, gazing off to their left.

On the dirty surface of a train window, faded, now illegible graffiti has been scrawled in the dust. Blurred, abstract shapes move across it.

Slowly the focus shifts, defining the shapes as details of the passing landscape. Overgrown fields dwarf a simple wooden farmhouse. The house floats out of view and the fields become forests. The forests are replaced by more fields, then rolling hills. The hills become flat plains. Several abandoned, broken conastoga wagons pass through the frame of the train window, their tattered canvas coverings flapping in the strong wind, thick weeds growing through their wheel spokes. Then more woods, which are again replaced by empty plains.

Chapter Credits By Film Element

94. *Hedwig and the Angry Inch* (2001)

Writer:	John Cameron Mitchell (Screenplay & Play)
Writer:	Stephen Trask (Play music & lyrics)
Director:	John Cameron Mitchell
Production Company:	Killer Films
Production Company:	New Line Cinema
Distributor:	Fine Line Features (USA)
Distributor:	New Line Cinema

95. *The Sweet Hereafter* (1997)

Writer:	Atom Egoyan (Screenplay)
Writer:	Russel Banks (Novel)
Director:	Atom Egoyan
Production Company:	Alliance Communications Corporation
Production Company:	Canadian Film or Video Tax Credit
Production Company:	Ego Film Arts
Production Company:	Gort of Canada
Production Company:	The Harold Greenberg Fund
Production Company:	The Movie Network
Production Company:	Telefilm Canada
Distributor:	Alliance Communications Corporation
Distributor:	New Line Home Video (USA) (DVD)

96. *Blue Velvet* (1986)

Writer:	David Lynch
Director:	David Lynch
Production Company:	De Laurentiis
Distributor:	De Laurentiis

97. *Dead Man* (1995)

Writer:	Jim Jarmusch
Director:	Jim Jarmusch
Production Company:	12 Gauge Productions
Production Company:	JVC Entertainment
Production Company:	Pandora Film Produktion GmbH
Production Company:	Miramax
Distributor:	Miramax

SECTION **17** NATURAL
ENVIRONMENT

NATURAL ENVIRONMENT

Nature offers endless storytelling options for dramatists. Think about what the desert adds to *Thelma and Louise*, the rain in *Blade Runner*, or the crashing waves in *From Here to Eternity*. Movies are designed to exploit sound and motion, and natural elements very easily provide these.

Natural Environment Might Be Divided into Four Groups:

For the sake of simplicity here's one way to categorize their dramatic potential.

1. Things that move;   2. Things that make sounds;

3. Things that add peril;   4. Things that can serve as metaphor.

1. Things That Move

Movies are designed to exploit motion. Nature provides visually spectacular moving elements that can physically dramatize a scene. Snow, wind, and lightning, for example, can "comment" on a scene.

2. Things That Make Sounds

Most of the elements that move also make sound. They can an add an auditory story plane to any scene. For example, a hailstorm can drown out an important clue, or draw attention to it. Sound can creep into a scene or land with a bang.

3. Things That Add Peril

Nature can be seen as sanctuary or a source of destruction. The reason nature can supply an endless trove of plotlines is simple: It can give life or take it away with ease. In Von Stroheim's classic film, *Greed*, we learn the true nature of two men as they battle to their death in an arid desert over a single canteen of water.

4. Natural Elements That Serve as Metaphors

Metaphors can be created from any element and nature is one source to consider.
A blinding snowstorm in *Fargo*, for example, leaves Jerry Lundegard's windshield covered in ice. The ice-covered windshield might be seen as a metaphor for the character's inner blindness. The storm's sound and motion add drama to later scenes, while the ice-covered terrain reminds us of the ongoing threat of the environment.

A Comment on Metaphors

What makes nature so potent a source for metaphor is its power and unpredictability. As fire can represent the family hearth in one scene, it can bring death in the next. Like water, it can provide or destroy. Natural metaphors also a carry a sort of timeless authority.

Film Elements

In the following section, we look at three uses of nature. Though each is different, they all augment the scene by adding subtext and depth to the story.

98. Climate   *The Sixth Sense* (cold)

99. Seasons   *Amélie* (montage)

100. Physical Phenomenon   *Dolores Claiborne* (eclipse)

98. Film Element: Climate

Natural elements can raise the volume in a scene. They can amplify a character's action by creating a physical after effect. When Thelma and Louise's car spins around in the desert, a huge gust of sand whips up around the car exaggerating the moment. When Harrison Ford thrashes through water-filled, underground pipes in *The Fugitive*, each step sends up a huge splash and the sound of water.

The physical world is a great tool to exploit, and climate is but one of the options. It can be organic to the scene or used more theatrically depending on genre. In a brilliant use of "climate," writer M. Night Shyamalan uses "cold" to identify the presence of ghosts. Shyamalan gives the audience a visual clue with which to track the story progression in his phenomenal script, *The Sixth Sense*.

Film Example: *The Sixth Sense*

In the opening scene Shyamalan introduces us to the central clue in the movie. The protagonist's wife has gone down to the cellar to retrieve a bottle of wine. The audience doesn't suspect anything when the woman's breath forms a "tiny cloud of cold air." We assume it's because the basement is cold.

As the movie progresses we realize that coldness is very important. In fact, we soon notice that whenever a ghost shows up, the temperature drops. We then think back on some earlier scenes and reconsider their meaning. The audience makes these connections ahead of the protagonist. Not until the end of the movie does the protagonist understand that he is the cause of the "tiny clouds of cold air" forming from his wife's lips — and that he is dead.

Dramatic Value

Ghost movies, like all genre films, have to guard against predictability. Bringing new conventions to a well-developed form is difficult. *The Sixth Sense* does a brilliant job in reinventing the staples of the genre. In this instance it does so while giving the audience a useful visual device with which to track the developing plot.

The Sixth Sense (1999)

Screenplay: M. Night Shyamalan, Draft: May 1, 1998

Page 1

INT. BASEMENT - EVENING

Anna turns to leave. Stops. She stares at the shadowy basement.
It's an unsettling place. She stands very still and watches
her breath form a TINY CLOUD IN THE COLD AIR. She is visibly
uncomfortable.

Page 58

INT. COLE'S HOUSE - NIGHT

An unnatural silence fills each room of the house.

The thermostat on the wall now reads, fifty-two degrees.

Page 85

INT. HALL - NIGHT

Cole closes the door to his mother's bedroom shut. He stands

still in the hallway. Lets out a heavy sigh...

HIS BREATH ROLLS IN A TINY CLOUD IN FRONT OF HIM.

Cole's brow furrows. He breathes again. This time

intentionally. Watches as his breath materializes in the

suddenly ice cold air.

Page 104

CLOSE ON ANNA... TILL HER SLEEPING FACE FILLS THE FRAME...
IT'S NOW WE NOTICE FOR THE FIRST TIME, THAT ANNA'S BREATHS ARE
FORMING TINY CLOUDS IN THE COLD AIR.

MALCOLM

(like he's falling down a deep hole)

No...

1.

2.

3.

4.

99. Film Element: Seasons and the Passage of Time

In the beautiful film, *Amélie,* changing climate is used to illustrate the passage of time.

Film Example: *Amélie*

Amélie is a whimsical, five-year-old child who prefers to wait inside until the time to leave home. In illustrating the "wait period," a brief climate-driven montage spanning seventeen years takes place beneath Amélie's apartment window.

In the script, the passage of time is shown by the wear the years have made on Amélie's teddy bear. Although it remains in the four-shot montage, its disintegration alone may have been too hard to "'read" as the passage of time. In either case, seasonal change was added to the filmed montage which lends physical drama to the scene.

Dramatic Value

As seasonal changes are both visually distinctive and universal, audiences easily read them as representing the passage of time.

Amélie (2001) (Page 7)

Screenplay: Guillaume Laurent & Jean-Pierre Jeunet, 2001.

```
                    VOICE OVER
        The days, the months, the years go by.
        The outside world seems so dead that Amélie
        prefers to remain in her dream-life until the
        time comes for her to leave home.
```

Beneath the window, a teddy-bear belonging to the young Amélie lies forgotten on the lawn.

Years pass. The teddy-bear disintegrates, bit by bit.

When there's just a little of its stuffing left, a bird lands next to the bear, picks up the morsel of stuffing in its beak and flies away.

1.

2.

3.

4.

100. Film Element: Physical Phenomena

When thunder strikes at the beginning of a character's journey it is like nature signaling that peril lies ahead. In this way nature can comment on a story as it unfolds. Nature is put to such a use in *Dolores Claiborne*. Here nature lends a supportive nod confirming for Dolores the "rightness" of the murder she has just committed.

Film Example: *Dolores Claiborne*

Dolores Claiborne is about a woman who kills her husband. For practical reasons she waits for the highly anticipated eclipse to do the deed. The eclipse will vacate the small island she lives on, as everyone will go to the mainland to celebrate. The fireworks and festivities over the water will also mask any sound.

From the start of the film the eclipse is planted as organic to the story landscape. Once established it can be fully exploited artistically.

The murder occurs when Dolores leads her husband on a chase. The chase is orchestrated so that he will fall to his death. Each stage of the chase shows us the changing stages of the eclipse. Finally as her husband crashes to his death, the eclipse, like a messenger of nature, visually confirms for Dolores that what she has done is right. The moon passes across the sun, leaving the sun in darkness, and then the sun slowly reemerges, saturating the scene with a golden glow. It's an exquisite metaphor for the light returning to Dolores' life.

Dramatic Value

Here nature serves two jobs dramatically. First, the event of the eclipse, and the darkness that follows, facilitates the murder. In this way nature physically lends support to the character's deed. It then floods her with light, morally interpreting and condoning her action, playing the role of a spiritual guide.

Script Note

The script contained numerous references to the upcoming eclipse. The five excerpts on the next page are brief extracts from the murder sequence. The extensive frame grabs are included to demonstrate how beautifully the film was able to harness nature to aid in the storytelling.

Dolores Claiborne (1995)

Screenplay: Tony Gilroy, Third Draft 3/11/94.
Based on the novel by Stephen King.

Dolores preparing herself for the murder (Page 102)

THE KITCHEN. Dolores standing there, watching the water just run. Horns of a dilemma. Steeling herself.

OUT THE WINDOW

THE SKY. An odd cast to it. The clouds have burned away. A strange, thin, rose tint starting to develop. HORNS on the boats starting to echo more frequently on the wind.

     JOE (OS)
   Well, here we go.

Joe throwing Dolores to the ground (Page 104)

     DOLORES
    (eyes casting above)

 ... my God, lookit that... Stars.

THE SKY -- She's right. Stars twinkling against an ethereal purple background. A strange, accelerated sunset. The sun being swallowed by a huge, black, full moon.

Joe pursues Dolores (Page 106)

Suddenly, it's a chase --- Dolores out front -- ten yards ahead -- sprinting off the driveway and into the field -- Joe's gaining ground -- stumbling in the darkness -- but even drunk he's faster than she is --

Joe falls as Dolores hoped (Page 107)

THE SKY. Total eclipse. A thin wafer of brilliant light exploding from behind the moon's silhouette. Spectacular and clear. An exact moment. Beyond description.

Joe Dies (Page 110)

DOLORES standing now. Staring back over the field. As the light begins to return. As the sounds of the party boats and the birds begin to bleed back in. She looks down the well --

JOE'S BODY at the bottom. Bent and broken. He's dead.

1.

2.

3.

4.

(continues)

5.

6.

7.

8.

9.

10.

11.

12.

13.

14.

15.

16.

17.

18.

19.

20.

21.

22.

23.

24.

25.

26.

27.

27.

Chapter Credits By Film Element

98. *The Sixth Sense* (1999)

Writer:	M. Night Shyamalan
Director:	M. Night Shyamalan
Production Company:	Hollywood Pictures
Production Company:	Spyglass Entertainment
Production Company:	The Kennedy/Marshall Company
Distributor:	Buena Vista

99. *Amélie* (2001)

Writer:	Guillame Laurant, Jean-Pierre Jeunet (Screenplay)
Writers:	Guillame Laurant, Jean-Pierre Jeunet (Story)
Director:	Jean-Pierre Jeunet
Production Company:	Filmstiftung Nordhein-Westfalen
Production Company:	France 3 Cinema
Production Company:	La Sofica Sofinergie 5
Production Company:	Le Studio Canal+
Production Company:	MMC Independent GmblH
Production Company:	Tapioca Films
Production Company:	UGC Images
Production Company:	Victories Productions
Distributor:	Miramax

100. *Dolores Claiborne* (1995)

Writer:	Tony Gilroy (Screenplay)
Writer:	Stephen King (Novel)
Director:	Taylor Hackford
Production Company:	Castle Rock Entertainment
Production Company:	Columbia Pictures Corporation
Distributor:	Columbia Pictures

NOTE ON CREDITS AND SCRIPT SOURCES

For consistency, credits were taken from www.IMDbPro.com. Although every effort was made to properly credit sources, if any errors or omissions occurred, please contact the author.

Script Sources
As scripts are rarely produced in book form, scripts were culled from a variety of sources. Here's the list.

1. Published works
2. J. Paul Leonard Library, San Francisco State University, Reserve Room
3. Screenstyle; see *moviescriptsoncd.com*
4. Script City, Los Angeles
5. Hollywood Book & Poster, Los Angeles
6. Limelight Books, San Francisco
7. Internet sites

Script Excerpts
In this book you will see two kinds of scripts: published and unpublished.

Published and Unpublished Scripts
The difficulty in using published scripts is that they are intended for the general public. They are either the final shooting script or are directly transcribed from the screen. This makes it hard for the student of screenwriting to see where the writer stops and the director starts, as the director naturally contributes changes. The earlier unpublished writer's drafts allow readers to better evaluate what the screenwriter contributes and how they express cinematic story ideas as writers.

The unpublished screenplay is also valuable because the format has not been altered for publication needs. However, as works-in-progress they will not be as polished as the published screenplays and will never match the final movie perfectly, they are often significantly altered. A few examples of this have been included to make the point that scripts are continually reshaped during both the writing and production process. It is our fortune that these unpublished screenplays have been made available to be studied.

When a published script is also available the publisher is listed under the Script Sources section under Published Screenplay Available or PSA. The reader is encouraged to compare the earlier unpublished drafts of the screenplay to the published shooting script and evaluate the changes made. A lot can be learned by these comparisons.

Editing Scripts
In most cases I have left the writer's version untouched. In a few cases I have added a slugline as some excerpts were taken mid-scene. I have occasionally corrected an obvious typographical error to help make the writer's meaning clear.

Script Sources
1. *Strangers on a Train* (Film Element 1)
Screenplay Credits: Czenzi Ormonde, Raymond Chandler
Draft: Final Draft: Oct. 18, 1950
Source: *www.screentalk.org*

2. *The Piano* (Film Element 3)
Screenplay Credit: Jane Campion
Draft: 4th Draft, 1991
Source: Screenstyle. See: *moviescriptsoncd.com*
Published Script Available: Miramax 1993

3. *Dolores Claiborne* (Film Element 5)
Screenplay Credit: Tony Gilroy
Draft: Third Draft, March 11, 1994.
Source: Script City

4. *The Graduate* (Film Element 6)
Screenplay Credits: Calder Willingham and Buck Henry.
Source: Thomas, Sam, Editor. *Best American Screenplays*, First Series, Complete Screenplays, Crown Publishers, Inc., New York, 1986, pages 296-336.

5. *Citizen Kane* (Film Element 7)
Screenplay Credit: Herman J. Mankiewicz and Orson Welles
Source: Thomas, Sam, Editor. *Best American Screenplays 2*, Complete Screenplays, Crown Publishers, Inc., New York, 1990, pages 7-81.

6. *Disco Pigs* (Film Element 8)
Screenplay Credit: Enda Walsh
Source: Script donated by Kirsten Sheridan (director).

7. *Disco Pigs* (Film Element 9)
Screenplay Credit: Enda Walsh
Source: Script donated by Kirsten Sheridan (director).

8. *The Conversation* (Film Element 12)
Screenlay Credit: Francis Coppola
Draft: November 11, 1972
Source: Script City

9. *Fargo* (Film Element 13)
Screenplay Credits: Joel Coen & Ethan Coen
Draft: November 2, 1994
Source: Script City
Published Script Available: Faber & Faber 1996

10. *Witness* (Film Element 14)
Screenplay Credits: William Kelley, Earl Wallace
Draft: Revised Draft, 1984
Source: Screenstyle. See: *moviescriptsoncd.com*

11. *The Searchers* (Film Element 15)
Screenplay: Frank Nugent
Draft: Revised Final Draft
Source: Script City

12. *Citizen Kane* (Film Element 17)
Screenplay: Herman J. Mankiewicz and Orson Welles
Source: Thomas, Sam, Editor. *Best American Screenplays 2*, Complete Screenplays, Crown Publishers, Inc., New York, 1990, pages 7-81.

13. *Adaptation* (Film Element 18)
Screenplay Credits: Charlie Kaufman and Donald Kaufman
Draft: November 21, 2000
Source: Screenstyle. See: *moviescriptsoncd.com*
Published Script Available: Newmarket Press 2003

14. *Psycho* (Film Element 19)
Screenplay Credit: Joseph Stephano
Draft: Revised Draft, December 1, 1959
Source: Screenstyle. See: *moviescriptsoncd.com*

15. *Psycho* (Film Element 20)
Same as above

16. *Cabaret* (Film Element 21)
Screenplay Credit: Jay Presson Allen
Draft: First Draft, June 7, 1970
Source: Script City

17. *Citizen Kane* (Film Element 23)
Screenplay: Herman J. Mankiewicz and Orson Welles
Source: Thomas, Sam, Editor. *Best American Screenplays 2*, Complete Screenplays, Crown Publishers, Inc., New York, 1990, pages 7-81

18. *American Beauty* (Film Element 25)
Screenplay Credit: Alan Ball
Draft: April 1, 1998
Source: Script City
Published Script Available: Newmarket Press 2000

19. *Barton Fink* (Film Element 24)
Screenplay Credits: Joel Coen and Ethan Coen
Draft: Feb. 19, 1990.
Source: Script City
Published Script Available: Faber & Faber 1991

20. *Pulp Fiction* (Film Element 27)
Screenplay Credit
Stories by: Quentin Tarantino & Roger Avary
Draft: May, 1993
Source: Script City
Published Script Available: Hyperion 1994.

21. *Pulp Fiction* (Film Element 28)
Same as above
Published Script Available: Hyperion 1994.

22. *Raging Bull* (Film Element 29)
Screenplay Credits: Paul Shrader and Mardik Martin
Draft: Not Dated. Movie Released in 1980.
Screenstyle. See: *moviescriptsoncd.com*

23. *Sunset Boulevard* (Film Element 31)
Screenplay Credits: Charles Brackett, Billy Wilder, D.M. Marshman, Jr.

Draft: March 21, 1949
Source: Script City

24. *The People vs. Larry Flynt* (Film Element 32)
Screenplay Credits: Scott Alexander & Larry Karaszewski
Draft: Revised First Draft, 1994
Published Script Available: Newmarket Press 1996

25. *Butch Cassidy and the Sundance Kid* (Film Element 33)
Screenplay Credit: William Goldman
Thomas, Sam, Editor. *Best American Screenplays*, First Series, Complete Screenplays, Crown Publishers, Inc., New York, 1986, pages 337-391.

26. *The Piano* (Film Element 34)
Screenplay Credit: Jane Campion
Draft: 4th Draft, 1991
Source: Screenstyle. See: *moviescriptsoncd.com*
Published Script Available: Miramax 1993

27. *Klute* (Film Element 35)
Screenplay Credit: Andy Lewis, Dave Lewis
Draft: 1971
Source: Script City

28. *ET* (Film Element 36)
Screenplay Credit: Melissa Mathison
Draft: Sept 8, 1991, Shooting Script
Source: Script City

29. *Barton Fink* (Film Element 37)
Screenplay Credits: Joel Coen and Ethan Coen
Draft: Feb. 19, 1990.
Source: Script City
Published Script Available: Faber & Faber 1991

30. *Barton Fink* (Film Element 38)
Same as above
Published Script Available: Faber & Faber 1991

31. *Apocalypse Now* (Film Element 39)
Screenplay Credits: John Milius and Francis Coppola

This excerpt is from a *transcript* of the movie, the lyrics were not included in the original screenplay.
Source: Screenstyle. See: *moviescriptsoncd.com*
Published Script Available: Miramax 2001

32. *Shawshank Redemption* (Film Element 40)
Screenplay Credit: Frank Darabont
Draft: 1994
Source: Screenstyle. See: *moviescriptsoncd.com*
Published Script Available: Newmarket Press 2004

33. *Out of Africa* (Film Element 41)
Screenplay Credit: Kurt Luedke
Draft: August, 1983
Source: Script City

34. *Sorry, Wrong Number* (Film Element 42)
Screenplay Credit: Lucille Fletcher
This excerpt is from the published play written by Lucille Fletcher.
Source: Fletcher, Lucille. *Sorry, Wrong Number* and *The Hitchhiker*, Dramatists Play Service, Inc., New York, 1952, copyright renewed, 1980.

35. *Barton Fink* (Film Element 44)
Screenplay Credits: Joel Coen and Ethan Coen
Draft: Feb. 19, 1990.
Source: Script City
Published Script Available: Faber & Faber 1991

36. *Single White Female* (Film Element 45)
Screenplay Credit: Don Roos
Draft: August 9, 1991
Source: Script City

37. *Citizen Kane* (Film 46)
Screenplay: Herman J. Mankiewicz and Orson Welles
Source: Thomas, Sam, Editor. *Best American Screenplays 2*, Complete Screenplays, Crown Publishers, Inc., New York, 1990, pages 7-81

38. *Harold and Maude* (Film Element 49)
Screenplay Credit: Colin Higgins

Draft: 1971
Source: Hollywood Book & Poster

39. *Titanic* (Film Element 50)
Screenplay Credit: James Cameron
Draft: May 7, 1966, Revised
Source: Script City
Published Script Available: HarperEnt. 1998

40. *Bound* (Film Element 51)
Screenplay Credits: Larry Wachowski & Andy Wachowski
Draft: First Draft, September 28, 1994.
Source: Script City

41. *Citizen Kane* (Film Element 52)
Screenplay: Herman J. Mankiewicz and Orson Welles
Source: Thomas, Sam, Editor. *Best American Screenplays 2*, Complete Screenplays, Crown Publishers, Inc., New York, 1990, pages 7-81

42. *The Piano* (Film Element 53)
Screenplay Credit: Jane Campion
Draft: 4th Draft, 1991
Source: Screenstyle. See: *moviescriptsoncd.com*
Published Script Available: Miramax 1993

43. *Citizen Kane* (Film Element 56)
Screenplay: Herman J. Mankiewicz and Orson Welles
Source: Thomas, Sam, Editor. *Best American Screenplays 2*, Complete Screenplays, Crown Publishers, Inc., New York, 1990, pages 7-81

44. *The Piano* (Film Element 60)
Screenplay Credit: Jane Campion
Draft: 4th Draft, 1991
Source: Screenstyle. See: *moviescriptsoncd.com*
Published Script Available: Miramax 1993

45. *Halloween* (Film Element 62)
Screenplay Credit: John Carpenter and Debra Hill
Draft: Final Draft. Not dated. Movie released in 1978.
Source: Screenstyle. See: *moviescriptsoncd.com*

46. *Jaws* (Film Element 63)
Screenplay Credit: Peter Benchley and Carl Gottlieb
Draft: Final Draft. Draft not dated. Movie released in 1975.
Source: Screenstyle. See: *moviescriptsoncd.com*

47. *Citizen Kane* (Film Element 64)
Screenplay: Herman J. Mankiewicz and Orson Welles
Source: Thomas, Sam, Editor. *Best American Screenplays 2*, Complete Screenplays, Crown Publishers, Inc., New York, 1990, pages 7-81

48. *ET* (Film Element 64)
Screenplay Credit: Melissa Mathison
Draft: Sept 8, 1991, Shooting Script
Source: Script City

49. *ET* (Film Element 65)
Same as above

50. *Psycho* (Film Element 66)
Screenplay Credit: Joseph Stephano
Draft: Revised Draft, December 1, 1959
Source: Screenstyle. See: *moviescriptsoncd.com*

51. *Klute* (Film Element 67)
Screenplay Credit: Andy Lewis, Dave Lewis
Draft: 1971
Source: Script City

52. *The Professional* (Film Element 69)
Screenplay Credit: Luc Besson
Draft: Seaside, 1993
Source: Script City

53. *Fargo* (Film Element 70)
Screenplay Credits: Joel Coen & Ethan Coen
Draft: November 2, 1994
Source: Script City
Published Script Available: Faber & Faber 1996

54. *Bound* (Film Element 71)
Screenplay Credits: Larry Wachowski & Andy Wachowski

Draft: First Draft, September 28, 1994.
Source: Script City

55. *Fargo* (Film Element 74)
Screenplay Credits: Joel Coen & Ethan Coen
Draft: November 2, 1994
Source: Script City
Published Script Available: Faber & Faber 1996

56. *Touch of Evil* (Film Element 76)
Screenplay Credits: Orson Welles
Draft: Rev. Final Screenplay, Feb. 5, 1957
Source: Script City

57. *Pulp Fiction* (Film Element 77)
Screenplay Credit: Quentin Tarantino
Stories by: Quentin Tarantino & Roger Avary
Draft: May, 1993
Source: Script City
Published Script Available: Hyperion 1994

58. *Goodfellas* (Film Element 78)
Screenplay Credit: Nicolas Pileggi & Martin Scorsese
Draft: January 12, 1989
This draft credited to Nicolas Pileggi.
Source: *www.dailyscript.com*
Published Script Available: Faber & Faber 1990

59. *The Piano* (Film Element 79)
Screenplay Credit: Jane Campion
Draft: 4th Draft, 1991
Source: Screenstyle. See: *moviescriptsoncd.com*
Published Script Available: Miramax 1993

60. *Natural Born Killers* (Film Element 81)
Screenplay Credit: David Veloz (Screenplay) & Richard Rutowski (Screenplay) &
Oliver Stone (Screenplay), Quentin Tarantino (Story)
Draft: Draft Five, May 11, 1993
Credits for this draft: Quentin Tarantino, David Veloz, Richard Rutowski, and Oliver Stone. In the final film credits, Quentin Tarantino received "story" credit.

Source: Screenstyle. See: *moviescriptsoncd.com*
Published Script Available: Grove Press 2000

61. *American Beauty* (Film Element 82)
Screenplay Credit: Alan Ball
Draft: April 1, 1998.
Source: Script City
Published Script Available: Newmarket Press 2000

62. *The Professional* (Film Element 84)
Screenplay Credit: Luc Besson
Draft: Seaside, 1993
Source: Script City

63. *ET* (Film Element 85)
Screenplay Credit: Melissa Mathison
Draft: Sept 8, 1991, Shooting Script
Source: Script City

64. *Barton Fink* (Film Element 87)
Screenplay Credits: Joel Coen and Ethan Coen
Draft: Feb. 19, 1990.
Source: Script City
Published Script Available: Faber & Faber 1991

65. *Raging Bull* (Film Element 88)
Screenplay Credits: Paul Shrader and Mardik Martin
Draft: Not Dated. Movie Released in 1980.
Source: Screenstyle. See: *moviescriptsoncd.com*

66. *Harold and Maude* (Film Element 90)
Screenplay Credit: Colin Higgins
Draft: 1971
Source: Hollywood Book & Poster Co

67. *Ed Wood* (Film Element 91)
Screenplay Credit: Scott Alexander & Larry Karaszewsi
Draft: First Draft, November 20, 1992.
Published Script Available: Faber & Faber 1995

68. *Out of Africa* (Film Element 92)
Screenplay Credit: Kurt Luedke
Draft: August, 1983

Source: Script City

69. *Bound* (Film Element 93)
Screenplay Credits: Larry Wachowski & Andy Wachowski
Draft: First Draft, September 28, 1994.
Source: Script City

70. *Hedwig and the Angry Inch* (Film Element 94)
Screenplay Credit: John Cameron Mitchell
Draft: Revised January 3, 2000
Source: Hollywood Book and Poster Co.

71. *The Sweet Hereafter* (Film Element 95)
Screenplay Credit: Atom Egoyan
Draft: Final Revised Draft, 1997
Source: *www.dailyscript.com*

72. *Blue Velvet* (Film Element 96)
Screenplay Credit: David Lynch
Draft: Final Script, 1986
Source: Screenstyle. See: *moviescriptsoncd.com*

73. *Dead Man* (Film Element 97)
Screenplay Credit: Jim Jarmusch
Draft: February 21, 1994
Source: Hollywood Book & Poster Co.
Published Script Available: Newmarket Press 1997

74. *The Sixth Sense* (Film Element 98)
Screenplay Credit: M. Night Shyamalan
Draft: May 1, 1998
Source: Script City

75. *Amélie* (Film Element 99)
Screenplay Credit: Guillaume Laurent & Jean-Pierre Jeunet
Draft: Not Dated. Movie Released in 2001
Source: Limelight, San Francisco

76. *Dolores Claiborne* (Film Element 100)
Screenplay Credit: Tony Gilroy
Draft: Third Draft, March 11, 1994.
Source: Script City

REFERENCES

Altman, Robert. "Commentary: Robert Altman." Interview with Robert Altman. DVD release of *Three Women* (20th Century Fox, 1977). Criterion Collection, 2004.

Arnheim, Rudolph. *Art and Visual Perception*. Berkeley: University of California Press, 1954.

———. *Visual Thinking*. Berkeley: University of California Press, 1969.

Block, Bruce. *The Visual Story: Seeing the Structure of Film, TV, and New Media*. Boston: Focal Press, 2000.

Coppola, Francis. "Commentary. Francis Coppola." Interview by Peter Horner. DVD release of *The Conversation* (Paramount, 1974). American Zoetrope, 2000.

Eisenstein, Sergei. "Dickens, Griffith and Film Today." *Film Theory and Criticism: Introductory Readings*. 4th edition. Edited by Gerald Mast, Marshall Cohen and Leo Braudy. London: Oxford University Press, 1992. 395-402.

———. *Film Form: Essays in Film Theory*. Edited and translated by Jay Leyda. New York: Harcourt Brace & Co., 1949 (1977).

Hitchcock, Alfred. *A Talk with Hitchcock*. A Telescope interview with Fletcher Markle. Canadian Broadcasting Production, 1964.

Jesionowski, Joyce E. *Thinking in Pictures*. Berkeley: University of California Press, 1987.

Kuleshov, Lev. *Kuleshov on Film 1922-1968*. Translated and edited with an introduction by Ronald Levaco. Berkeley: University of California Press, 1974.

Lumet, Sidney. *Making Movies*. New York: Alfred A. Knopf, 1995.

Mast, Gerald, Marshall Cohen and Leo Braudy, ed. *Film Theory and Criticism: Introductory Readings*. 4th edition. London: Oxford University Press, 1992.

Pudovkin, Vsevolod. *Film Technique and Film Acting*. New York: Grove Press, 1970.

———. "On Editing." *Film Theory and Criticism: Introductory Readings*. 4th edition. Edited by Gerald Mast, Marshall Cohen and Leo Braudy. Oxford University Press, 1992. 121-26.

CREDITS FOR SECTION IMAGES

Page	Section	Movie Credit
1	1	*Citizen Kane*
17	2	*Metropolis*
31	3	*The Searchers*
45	4	*Psycho*
67	5	*Metropolis*
89	6	*Barton Fink*
101	7	*The Piano*
109	8	*Fatal Attraction*
133	9	*Requiem for a Dream*
147	10	*Kill Bill Vol. 1*
167	11	*The 400 Blows*
195	12	*Apocalypse Now*
209	13	*Three Women*
213	14	*Barton Fink*
223	15	*Harold and Maude*
231	16	*Blue Velvet*
241	17	*Dolores Claiborne*

ABOUT THE AUTHOR

Jennifer van Sijll teaches screenwriting at San Francisco State. She has an MFA from USC's Department of Cinema-Television. She has written story outlines for primetime television, and a successful children's pilot for PBS starring Pat Morita. She has worked as a script analyst for Universal Pictures, independent producers, and pay television. In 1994, she won the Panavision New Filmmaker award. In 1995, she was named honorary Gilliand Chair at San Jose State for teaching excellence.

Jennifer has taught intensive weekend scriptwriting courses for UC Berkeley for six years. Her courses have been featured on television programs including Talkin' Pictures. Jennifer regularly consults on film and television projects in Los Angeles and San Francisco. For information on seminars, consulting, and the upcoming DVD version of *Cinematic Storytelling*, please visit www.cinematicstorytelling.com.

MICHAEL WIESE PRODUCTIONS

Since 1981, Michael Wiese Productions has been dedicated to providing both novice and seasoned filmmakers with vital information on all aspects of filmmaking. We have published more than 70 books, used in over 500 film schools and countless universities, and by hundreds of thousands of filmmakers worldwide.

Our authors are successful industry professionals who spend innumerable hours writing about the hard stuff: budgeting, financing, directing, marketing, and distribution. They believe that if they share their knowledge and experience with others, more high quality films will be produced.

And that has been our mission, now complemented through our new web-based resources. We invite all readers to visit www.mwp.com to receive free tipsheets and sample chapters, participate in forum discussions, obtain product discounts — and even get the opportunity to receive free books, project consulting, and other services offered by our company.

Our goal is, quite simply, to help you reach your goals. That's why we give our readers the most complete portal for filmmaking knowledge available — in the most convenient manner.

We truly hope that our books and web-based resources will empower you to create enduring films that will last for generations to come.

Let us hear from you at anytime.

Sincerely,
Michael Wiese
Publisher, Filmmaker

www.mwp.com

FILM & VIDEO BOOKS

Cinematic Storytelling: *The 100 Most Powerful Film Conventions Every Filmmaker Must Know* / Jennifer Van Sijll / $24.95

Complete DVD Book, The: *Designing, Producing, and Marketing Your Independent Film on DVD* / Chris Gore and Paul J. Salamoff / $26.95

Complete Independent Movie Marketing Handbook, The: *Promote, Distribute & Sell Your Film or Video* / Mark Steven Bosko / $39.95

Costume Design 101: *The Business and Art of Creating Costumes for Film and Television* / Richard La Motte / $19.95

Could It Be a Movie?: *How to Get Your Ideas Out of Your Head and Up on the Screen* / Christina Hamlett / $26.95

Creating Characters: *Let Them Whisper Their Secrets* Marisa D'Vari / $26.95

Crime Writer's Reference Guide, The: *1001 Tips for Writing the Perfect Crime* Martin Roth / $20.95

Cut by Cut: *Editing Your Film or Video* Gael Chandler / $35.95

Digital Filmmaking 101: *An Essential Guide to Producing Low-Budget Movies* Dale Newton and John Gaspard / $24.95

Digital Moviemaking, 2nd Edition: *All the Skills, Techniques, and Moxie You'll Need to Turn Your Passion into a Career* / Scott Billups / $26.95

Directing Actors: *Creating Memorable Performances for Film and Television* Judith Weston / $26.95

Directing Feature Films: *The Creative Collaboration Between Directors, Writers, and Actors* / Mark Travis / $26.95

Eye is Quicker, The: *Film Editing; Making a Good Film Better* Richard D. Pepperman / $27.95

Fast, Cheap & Under Control: *Lessons Learned from the Greatest Low-Budget Movies of All Time* / John Gaspard / $26.95

Film & Video Budgets, 4th Updated Edition Deke Simon and Michael Wiese / $26.95

Film Directing: Cinematic Motion, 2nd Edition Steven D. Katz / $27.95

Film Directing: Shot by Shot, *Visualizing from Concept to Screen* Steven D. Katz / $27.95

Film Director's Intuition, The: *Script Analysis and Rehearsal Techniques* Judith Weston / $26.95

Film Production Management 101: *The Ultimate Guide for Film and Television Production Management and Coordination* / Deborah S. Patz / $39.95

Filmmaking for Teens: *Pulling Off Your Shorts* Troy Lanier and Clay Nichols / $18.95

First Time Director: *How to Make Your Breakthrough Movie* Gil Bettman / $27.95

From Word to Image: *Storyboarding and the Filmmaking Process* Marcie Begleiter / $26.95

Hitting Your Mark, 2nd Edition: *Making a Life – and a Living – as a Film Director* Steve Carlson / $22.95

Hollywood Standard, The: *The Complete and Authoritative Guide to Script Format and Style* / Christopher Riley / $18.95

I Could've Written a Better Movie Than That!: *How to Make Six Figures as a Script Consultant even if You're not a Screenwriter* / Derek Rydall / $26.95

Independent Film Distribution: *How to Make a Successful End Run Around the Big Guys* / Phil Hall / $24.95

Independent Film and Videomakers Guide – 2nd Edition, The: *Expanded and Updated* / Michael Wiese / $29.95

Inner Drives: *How to Write and Create Characters Using the Eight Classic Centers of Motivation* / Pamela Jaye Smith / $26.95

I'll Be in My Trailer!: *The Creative Wars Between Directors & Actors* John Badham and Craig Modderno / $26.95

Moral Premise, The: *Harnessing Virtue & Vice for Box Office Success* Stanley D. Williams, Ph.D. / $24.95

Myth and the Movies: *Discovering the Mythic Structure of 50 Unforgettable Films* / Stuart Voytilla / $26.95

On the Edge of a Dream: *Magic and Madness in Bali* Michael Wiese / $16.95

Perfect Pitch, The: *How to Sell Yourself and Your Movie Idea to Hollywood* Ken Rotcop / $16.95

Power of Film, The Howard Suber / $27.95

Psychology for Screenwriters: *Building Conflict in your Script* William Indick, Ph.D. / $26.95

Save the Cat!: *The Last Book on Screenwriting You'll Ever Need* Blake Snyder / $19.95

Screenwriting 101: *The Essential Craft of Feature Film Writing* Neill D. Hicks / $16.95

Screenwriting for Teens: *The 100 Principles of Screenwriting Every Budding Writer Must Know* / Christina Hamlett / $18.95

Script-Selling Game, The: *A Hollywood Insider's Look at Getting Your Script Sold and Produced* / Kathie Fong Yoneda / $16.95

Selling Your Story in 60 Seconds: *The Guaranteed Way to get Your Screenplay or Novel Read* / Michael Hauge / $12.95

Setting Up Your Scenes: *The Inner Workings of Great Films* Richard D. Pepperman / $24.95

Setting Up Your Shots: *Great Camera Moves Every Filmmaker Should Know* Jeremy Vineyard / $19.95

Shaking the Money Tree, 2nd Edition: *The Art of Getting Grants and Donations for Film and Video Projects* / Morrie Warshawski / $26.95

Sound Design: *The Expressive Power of Music, Voice, and Sound Effects in Cinema* / David Sonnenschein / $19.95

Stealing Fire From the Gods, 2nd Edition: *The Complete Guide to Story for Writers & Filmmakers* / James Bonnet / $26.95

Storyboarding 101: *A Crash Course in Professional Storyboarding* James Fraioli / $19.95

Ultimate Filmmaker's Guide to Short Films, The: *Making It Big in Shorts* Kim Adelman / $16.95

What Are You Laughing At?: *How to Write Funny Screenplays, Stories, and More* / Brad Schreiber / $19.95

Working Director, The: *How to Arrive, Thrive & Survive in the Director's Chair* Charles Wilkinson / $22.95

Writer's Journey, – 2nd Edition, The: *Mythic Structure for Writers* Christopher Vogler / $24.95

Writer's Partner, The: *1001 Breakthrough Ideas to Stimulate Your Imagination* Martin Roth / $24.95

Writing the Action Adventure: *The Moment of Truth* Neill D. Hicks / $14.95

Writing the Comedy Film: *Make 'Em Laugh* Stuart Voytilla and Scott Petri / $14.95

Writing the Killer Treatment: *Selling Your Story Without a Script* Michael Halperin / $14.95

Writing the Second Act: *Building Conflict and Tension in Your Film Script* Michael Halperin / $19.95

Writing the Thriller Film: *The Terror Within* Neill D. Hicks / $14.95

Writing the TV Drama Series: *How to Succeed as a Professional Writer in TV* Pamela Douglas / $24.95

DVD & VIDEOS

Field of Fish: *VHS Video* Directed by Steve Tanner and Michael Wiese, Written by Annamaria Murphy / $9.95

Hardware Wars: *DVD* / Written and Directed by Ernie Fosselius / $14.95

Sacred Sites of the Dalai Lamas – DVD, The: *A Pilgrimage to Oracle Lake* A Documentary by Michael Wiese / $22.95

To Order go to *www.mwp.com* or Call 1-800-833-5738